Creating an Award-Winning School

PRAISE FOR
CREATING AN AWARD-WINNING SCHOOL: OUTSIDE-THE-BOX THINKING FOR INSIDE-THE-SCHOOL SUCCESS

Wow! A book that gives you confidence and guides you through your early years as a building administrator and beyond. This book is easy to read and is organized in a way that the reader can quickly reference any topic. A must have for every administrator's library. As a past recipient of the Ohio Assistant Principal of the Year, I am asked for a recommendation of a great book for beginning administrators, well, wait no longer! This book has it all! It will guide you through your mission and purpose. Topics from summer planning to communications to taking care of yourself. I commend Dr. Walker and Dr. Litzel on this effort and thank them for sharing their wisdom. This must have book will serve you well now and for years to come.

Dr. Brian Bontempo
Superintendent of Auburn Career Center, Concord, Ohio
Educator for 33 years (20 years as a building administrator)

"The role of a school principal is challenging and can be overwhelming. This is a book that can help with those day to day challenges and is for all school administrators. Dr. Walker and Dr. Litzel provides 'out of the box' ideas to aid in the daily duties of being a school administrator. This book is an easy read that focuses on oneself, others, organization, operations, and outreach. These components are essential for the success of any building leader."

T.J. Ebert
Educator for 20 years, building administrator for 15 years,
2016 Hall of Fame School, 2018 Ohio Elementary principal of the Year

"As an elementary school principal, I found this book to be practical and user-friendly, giving school administrators checklists and other resources to make their multi-dimensional job a little bit easier! If you put this book's outside-the-box ideas into action, you can undoubtedly expect a positive school culture and in-school success!"

Jennifer Filomena
Building Principal
Ellsworth Hill Elementary School, Hudson, Ohio

Creating an Award-Winning School

Outside the Box Thinking for Inside-the-School Success

Janet M. Litzel & Joanie A. Walker

ROWMAN & LITTLEFIELD
Lanham • Boulder • New York • London

Published by Rowman & Littlefield

An imprint of The Rowman & Littlefield Publishing Group, Inc.
4501 Forbes Boulevard, Suite 200, Lanham, Maryland 20706
www.rowman.com

86–90 Paul Street, London EC2A 4NE

Copyright © 2021 by Janet M. Litzel and Joanie A. Walker

All rights reserved. No part of this book may be reproduced in any form or by any electronic or mechanical means, including information storage and retrieval systems, without written permission from the publisher, except by a reviewer who may quote passages in a review.

British Library Cataloguing in Publication Information Available

Library of Congress Cataloging-in-Publication Data
Names: Litzel, Janet M., 1948– author. | Walker, Joanie A., 1961– author.
Title: Creating an award-winning school : outside-the-box thinking for inside-the-school success / Janet M. Litzel & Joanie A. Walker.
Description: Lanham : Rowman & Littlefield, [2021] | Includes bibliographical references. | Summary: "Creating an Award-Winning School: Outside the Box Thinking for Inside-the-School Success, is the result of collaboration between the authors and practicing and retired administrators. The book is written for new and experienced school administrators, college level instructors, and leaders in the private sector. The authors designed the Principals' Professional Pyramid to serve as the foundation for the book. Creating the Pyramid and adapting the steps from the study of Steven Covey's Principle-Centered Leadership, the authors arranged the tasks of administration into five major steps. The steps are ONESELF, OTHERS, ORGANIZATION, and OPERATIONS and OUTREACH. The authors developed these steps because they felt that a principal should begin with ONESELF before dealing successfully with OTHERS. Once organization is implemented, then the principal can deal with the continued OPERATIONS of all the school. OUTREACH into a professional network is a necessity for the success of a building leader. Embedded in the book are suggestions of Outside the Box Thinking or practical ideas to enhance the day-to-day operations of the building leader. Field techniques, forms, charts, diagrams, and reflections offered by the authors. These have been used to support the topics and enhance the content for the reader"— Provided by publisher.
Identifiers: LCCN 2021033724 (print) | LCCN 2021033725 (ebook) | ISBN 9781475860832 (cloth) | ISBN 9781475860849 (paperback) | ISBN 9781475860856 (epub)
Subjects: LCSH: School improvement programs. | School principals. | Educational leadership. | School management and organization.
Classification: LCC LB2822.8 .L58 2021 (print) | LCC LB2822.8 (ebook) | DDC 371.2/07—dc23
LC record available at https://lccn.loc.gov/2021033724
LC ebook record available at https://lccn.loc.gov/2021033725

We are in awe of the courageous principals, teachers, support staff, students, and parents who have worked collaboratively throughout this pandemic year to keep schools open and learning at the forefront. This book is dedicated to their tireless efforts to ensure education continued regardless of the adversity.

Contents

Foreword	ix
Preface	xi
Acknowledgments	xiii
Introduction	1
1 Oneself: Developing Personal Traits and Strengths for Inside-the-School Success	5
2 Others: Developing Effective People Skills for Inside-the-School Success	21
3 Organization: Developing Systems and Schedules for Inside-the-School-Success	49
4 Operations: Developing the Processes that Operate Your School for Inside-the-School Success	73
5 Outreach: Developing Outside Networks and Gaining Effective Practices for Inside-the-School Success	91
Conclusion	109
Appendix A	117
Appendix B	119
Appendix C	137
Appendix D	145

References 151

About the Author 153

Foreword

I will never forget my first year of being a building principal. Twenty-seven years old, with four years of teaching experience. My initial assignment was in a K-12 building, where I was to serve as 7–12 principal, 7–12 athletic director, and in my free time was to coach football and advise the student council. To coin a popular phrase, "I didn't know what I didn't know." My success or failure was based entirely on my graduate school experience and the ability to create some mentor relationships with other nearby administrators. It was sink or swim.

My entire "indoctrination" received from the district administration was to receive a set of building keys and the order to be there at 7:00 a.m. on the following Monday. Things have certainly changed over the years, but there is a frightening piece of data indicating a high percentage of building administrators who leave the position within the initial few years on the job. The reasons for this are several: lack of effective in-service programs (local and state level), inability to lead others, frustration with the job, non-existent mentoring programs, perceived ineffectiveness in the position, lack of organizational skills, and the inability to create successful relationships within the school community. Seldom will you hear salary mentioned as a main factor in abandoning administration . . . it is the other issues. The success or failure of a school administrator is measured by the "climate" created in their building. Student learning is tied greatly to building climate. The great irony is that there are few graduate courses designed for fledgling administrators on HOW to create this climate. There have been books written, but many of those are based on philosophy and not practical or "hands-on." This book is different. Joanie and Janet have a vast level of successful experience as school administrators. They have been in the trenches and their noses have been bloodied.

Now, they are sharing their successes with new and experienced administrators on what to do, what not to do, and how to implement it.

Man, I could have used this book as a rookie principal!

Your success as a building administrator will be measured by others: parents, staff, community, board of education, etc. Your ability to do the right thing at the right time will ensure another contract. Your personal well-being and satisfaction with the job will hinge on those relationships. This book will not only discuss those necessary ingredients but will give you examples of HOW to get them done as well.

Do not be afraid. Our schools need leaders.

Ken Baker, Executive Director (retired)
Ohio Association of Secondary School Administrators (OASSA)
26-year veteran of school administration

Preface

WHO IS THIS WRITTEN FOR?

The book is written for school administrators new and experienced. The audience for this text could include college-level instructors in the areas of supervision and educational administration. There is also a market for training leaders in areas of business, medicine, sports, etc.

WHY WAS IT WRITTEN?

This book is the result of collaboration between the authors and multiple practicing and retired administrators in the field of education. The authors are retired school administrators from Award-Winning Schools with K-12 administrative experience. Sharing their experiences as principals, they also have extensive careers in higher education, teaching in the areas of educational leadership, organization and management, and curriculum and instruction.

In selecting the title for the book, the authors chose, *Creating an Award-Winning School, Outside the Box Thinking for Inside-the-School Success*. While efforts by the building principal may not necessarily lead to awards or global recognition, developing an effective school can lead to an award-winning atmosphere inside and outside the school. A positive internal school climate can help to develop a community awareness as to the efficacy of the overall school operations.

What can help to create this Award-Winning Atmosphere? Embedded in the book are suggestions of *Outside the Box Thinking* or practical ideas to enhance the day-to-day operations of the building principal. Reflection is an important part of Inside-the-School Success so following the suggestions and ideas is an opportunity for the reader to reflect and make applications of the material presented.

Dr. Janet M. Litzel has fifteen years of experience in elementary school and eleven years of experience in the middle level as a teacher and administrator. In addition, she has over twenty-five years of teaching and administrative experience at the college level serving as a member of the faculty for three universities. Dr. Litzel has been recognized by the Ohio Middle School Association on numerous occasions and as Ohio Middle Level Educator of the year in 2003.

Dr. Joanie A. Walker has thirty years of experience in secondary education, which includes nine years as a high school teacher and twenty-one years as a high school administrator. In addition, she is a current Professor of Practice in educational administration beginning her fifth year of service. Dr. Walker has earned several awards and was recognized by the Ohio Association of Secondary School Administrators (OASSA) as OASSA High School Principal of the year in 2006 and in 2013.

Having taught aspiring leaders at the college level, the authors felt that they had a responsibility to ensure the success of future school administrators. Therefore, their purpose for writing this book was to select relevant, timely topics in leadership and provide "out of the box" suggestions for new and experienced administrators. The goal was to provide guidance through organized checklists of techniques to enable administrators to be reflective, well-rounded principals to lead to successful "Award Winning Schools."

WHAT IS TO BE LEARNED

There is a great deal to be learned from this book because the text was designed to be used in a variety of ways. The building administrator can refer to the book daily. Checklists can be copied, shared, and used for the planning and implementation of many leadership tasks. The text can be used as a daily, weekly, or yearly support for the principal. The text can also be used as a reference for university classes, workshops, or staff development for administrators or leadership students.

Acknowledgments

This book has been compiled from a variety of experiences in the field of education in different grade levels, school buildings, and districts including higher education. The authors relied on interactions with practicing and retired administrators in the field of educational administration to support their writings. Due to the restrictions on travel during the pandemic, many long hours of phone calls had to be held between the authors to complete this book.

Special gratitude must be expressed to the persons who guided us on our writing journey. We would like to thank our readers in the field of administration who took time away from their daily endeavors to preread our text and offered valuable input: Andrea Anderson, Brian Bontempo, Dennis Holmes, Deb Howell, Jack Litzel, and Tony Loewer. Also, a huge thanks to our administrators who shared their thoughts to the readers in their endorsements: Brian Bontempo, T. J. Ebert, and Jennifer Filomena.

We would be remiss not to mention Megan Holzheimer, Jack Litzel, and Robin Nakon, our supporters in proofreading and technological editing. Without them, we could not have reached the end goal of a completed text. Special thanks to our friend and colleague, Ken Baker, who wrote the foreword for our book. Also, thanks should be given to our acquisition editor, Carly Wall, who offered her assistance in submitting our document to print.

While we wholeheartedly recognize this immediate support in completing our book, we also would like to credit the past teachers, principals, and central office personnel who have encouraged us along the way to become teachers and principals. In addition, these supportive educators included faculty at the graduate college level who encouraged us to seek our doctoral degrees and pursue an extended career in higher education teaching.

On a personal note, Dr. Litzel would like to thank her husband, Jack, for his support, proofreading, and handholding during this writing experience.

His patience through the writing process was commendable. Also, Dr. Litzel would like to acknowledge and thank her educational family members, Tera, Jen, Julie, Jill, and Jess, who serve as her tireless example of teaching and learning in the twenty-first century. She is in awe of their perseverance, creativity, drive, and interactions in helping our young people learn today.

Dr. Walker would also like to offer her deepest love and appreciation to her son Michael Murphy (Mikie) in heaven, son Mark, and daughter Megan for their unselfish attitude and support. Special thanks to Megan who has offered her expertise and guidance throughout this writing process. Her knowledge and expertise as an educator and graduate of an educational leadership program were invaluable.

Introduction

Having taught in the higher education setting, the authors designed the Principals' Professional Pyramid. This serves as the foundation for the book by arranging the topics and tasks of administrators into relevant steps. Creating the Pyramid and adapting the steps from the study of Steven Covey's Principle Centered Leadership,[1] the authors arranged the tasks of administration into five major steps.

The steps are ONESELF, OTHERS, ORGANIZATION, OPERATIONS, and OUTREACH. The authors developed these steps because they felt that a principal should begin with ONESELF before dealing successfully with OTHERS. Learning how to deal with those first two steps can help the principal to develop better ORGANIZATION. Once organization is implemented, then the principal can deal with the continued OPERATIONS of all the content from the previous steps.

An important part of this book is the inclusion of techniques and ideas from the current field of school administration. This section, entitled OUTREACH, is included to illustrate to principals the need for networking and the benefits of connecting to other administrators. The authors deemed it essential to incorporate suggestions and practices from principals, assistant principals, and district administrators to enhance the checklists and reflections presented in the book.

It is hopeful that by sharing methods currently used in the field of school administration, the authors will exemplify the checklist materials. It is important to note that a successful experience in the field of administration, especially for beginning principals, can be ensured through the development of a strong network.

HOW IS IT ORGANIZED?

There are five chapters included in the book. Each of the five chapters begins with an introduction to the topic on the title page. Multiple subtopics are presented under the main topic. Each topic begins with a rationale and is followed by a checklist of actions that can assist the principal in accomplishing tasks supporting the topic. At the end of the checklists are practical applications included in "Outside the Box Thinking." In addition, supporting the checklists are relevant forms and narrative reflections from the authors regarding their own experiences with the topic.

To begin the book, the Principals' Professional Pyramid is presented to serve as the basis for the organization of the content. This is an important part of the text as it serves as a guide for the reader. The structure exemplifies the numerous responsibilities of the principal in the role of instructional leader of the school.

THE PRINCIPALS' PROFESSIONAL PYRAMID

Steps to Organizing Tasks for School Administrators

The authors designed the *Principals' Professional Pyramid* to arrange the topics and tasks of administrators into relevant steps. The steps are ONESELF, OTHERS, ORGANIZATION, OPERATIONS, and OUTREACH. The authors developed these steps based on Principle Centered Leadership by Stephen Covey.[2] They felt that a principal should begin with *ONESELF* before dealing successfully with OTHERS. Learning how to deal with those first two steps can help the principal to develop better ORGANIZATION. Once organization is implemented, then the principal can deal with the continued OPERATIONS of all the content from the previous steps. Most importantly is the OUTREACH component and the ability to network to gain knowledge and support in the field. This pyramid is a continuum of interactions encouraging the principal to regularly reflect on all aspects of administration and most importantly, the principal's role in each.

ONESELF

Developing personal traits and strengths for Inside-the-School Success

OTHERS

Developing effective people skills for Inside-the-School Success

ORGANIZATION

Developing systems and schedules for Inside-the-School Success

OPERATIONS

Developing the processes that operate your school for Inside-the-School Success

OUTREACH

Developing outside networks and gaining effective practices for Inside-the-School Success

NOTES

1. Covey, Steven. *Principle-Centered Leadership* (New York: Fireside, 1992), 29–30.
2. Covey, *Principle-Centered Leadership*, 29–30.

Chapter 1

Oneself

Developing Personal Traits and Strengths for Inside-the-School Success

As administrators, it is important to develop traits for self-reflection, self-assessment, and self-confidence. The first topic, ONESELF, focuses on the inner well-being of principals as they lead the staff and students at the school. This is a powerful topic as it requires time to think about personal behavior, integrity, goal setting, problem-solving, school and community relations, and dealing with stress.

Reflective practices are essential for growth and development as a school administrator at any grade level. By placing this topic first, the authors are assisting in the development of strong traits for leadership. Throughout this section, principals will find examples and supportive narratives from the author's own personal experiences with the topics. Encouraging self-evaluation, an "Inside-the-School-Success," reflection sheet is included at the end of this topic for thoughts by the readers.

CONSISTENCY IN PERSONAL BEHAVIOR

RATIONALE: Before you even begin to work as a building principal, you need to analyze your own behavior as it affects others. Being in a leadership position requires consistency in personal behavior. This consistency can withstand scrutiny and help to invite confidence from your stakeholders. Working to establish your own leadership persona can lead to the development of personal and professional integrity. Follow the suggestions in the checklist below to build consistency in your own behavior.

1. Be careful when talking about people behind their backs. Your statements might make their way back to the person. This also creates distrust from people who hear you.

2. Apologize when you are wrong. Being quick to admit mistakes and adjust can promote trustworthiness from your stakeholders.
3. Be punctual. Respect your time and the time of others. Keep a calendar and watch or your phone alarm close at hand to help you with this task. Technology assistance such as google docs and google meet help to save time.
4. Confront people with care and respect. Listen carefully when spoken to. Practice these skills in your personal and professional interactions. Most people do not care what you say. But they do care that you listen to what they have to say.
5. Do not make promises you cannot keep. Do what you say you are going to do. If you cannot, let people know what is standing in your way.
6. Be thorough and conscientious. Write down your tasks and analyze strategies to complete them. Always ask for help when you feel overwhelmed or do not know the answer.
7. Build people up whenever you can. Recognize exemplary accomplishments. Be courteous and positive. Express a genuine interest in the families and lives of your employees. Set a good example.
8. Always attack the problem not the person. Use a systematic problem-solving model to reach solutions for yourself and with others. See *Outside the Box Thinking, the Problem-Solving Model* following this checklist.
9. Make decisions based on consistent values. Rely on sound principles of decision-making to maintain your objectivity.
10. Establish a mission statement for yourself to reflect the culture and climate of your school. Post this mission statement and share it with others. See *Outside the Box Thinking, Developing a Personal Mission Statement, and samples of Mission Statements* following this checklist.

OUTSIDE THE BOX THINKING
THE IDEAL PROBLEM-SOLVING MODEL

To develop strong traits for leadership, being consistent and handling stress are two important abilities. The principal can be confronted daily by complex problems that can result in emotionally driven solutions. Using a problem-solving model can assist the principal in keeping emotions out of decision-making. Steps need to be taken to break down complex issues and solve problems quickly and effectively. There are many problem-solving methods available and the leader can adjust to develop a system that fits his or her own personal needs. This model is a cycle that promotes systematic processing of

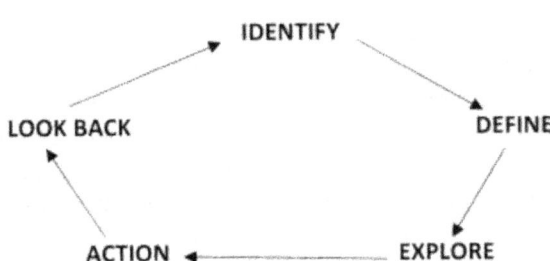

Figure 1.1. Above are the steps of the IDEAL model developed by Bransford and Stein. This model is a cycle of problem-solving.

issues and possible solutions to reach the best plan for resolution. Figure 1.1 includes the steps of the IDEAL model developed by Bransford and Stein.[1] This model is a cycle that promotes systematic processing of issues and possible solutions to reach the best plan for resolution.

STEPS IN THE IDEAL MODEL OF PROBLEM SOLVING

By Bransford and Stein

Problem-solving is a life skill that needs to be taught to adults. When encountering difficulties, whether it be among colleagues or with the public, it may become difficult to clearly define the problem. Without a systematic method for problem-solving, existing problems may never be successfully addressed. This model is effective to enable you to solve a variety of problems.

The components of the problem-solving model are represented by the acronym IDEAL. Each letter stands for an aspect of thinking that is important for problem-solving.

I   Identify Problem—Problem identification is often the most important step. This step is to recognize that a problem exists. A common reason for failure to identify problems is that people are often too emotionally involved in the problem to be able to really identify the exact issue.

D   Define Problem—There is a difference between problem identification and problem definition. Persons can agree on the existence of a problem but may disagree on a way to solve the problem. How the problem is defined will determine what alternatives are considered for the solution. This definition will lead to a difference in the solution chosen. Where there is a large amount of information about the problem, it may be necessary to use aids such as diagrams or charts to keep track of information. Once the problem is supported with definitions, it may be easier to explore options to solve the problem.

E Exploring Alternatives—This step involves brainstorming to create alternative solutions. Experienced problem solvers take a careful, systematic approach. This is a good strategy when the goal of the problem is clear. The best technique is to involve supporters in listening to possible solutions. The most important approach to exploring alternatives is to have a strong conceptual understanding of the area of the problem.

A L Act on the Plan—Look at Effects The first part of this step is to evaluate the strategies from the brainstorming session above. Determining which strategy will work may take some thought and contemplation. Evaluating strategies and determining who may implement them is part of the plan. Implementing the plan must have a specific amount of time. Evaluation of the plan should follow. Was enough time given for the strategy to work? Did the situation improve? If the strategy was unsuccessful, the problem solver should return to Exploring Alternatives and implement other alternatives and develop a new plan. This process should continue until the problem has been successfully solved.

Bransford, J., and Stein, B.[2]

OUTSIDE THE BOX THINKING
HOW TO IMPLEMENT THE PROBLEM-SOLVING MODEL

Before implementing any model, it is suggested that the leader explain the steps and practice the method with staff members. Modeling the process is essential to collaborative decision-making. Having everyone understand the model can assist the leader and staff with effective planning for problem resolution.

1. Begin by studying the steps of the model.
2. Then construct the problem that needs to be solved. Use the worksheet to help you.
3. Confer with other persons that might have insight into the issue for additional definition and alternatives to solving the problem. Brainstorm together and list all alternatives.
4. Then select the alternatives that would be most essential to solving the problem and then construct a plan.
5. With the plan, number the steps, designate who will complete each step, and the timeline to finish.

6. Finalize the plan and create a time frame for the completion of the steps. Then everyone involved must complete the steps assigned. Meet at the end of the time frame and evaluate the outcome.

SCENARIO

Mark is a new student at your school. He has transferred from a large city school district near you with passing grades. At the end of the first grading period, Mark is failing in all his major classes. However, he is receiving an A in computer and art classes. Mark's mother has called you, the principal, upset and wants some answers to help Mark.
- *How will you use the problem-solving model to help you, Mark, and his mother?*

IDENTIFY THE PROBLEM (Why is this your problem?)
- *The problem is that Mark's mother has called you to give her answers about Mark's grades.*

DEFINE THE PROBLEM (What factors contribute to the problem?)
- *Mark is a recent transfer from a larger school district.*
- *He is failing his major subjects after one grading period.*
- *His mother is surprised by his grades and is upset and wants help.*
- *He is getting A's in computer and art.*

EXPLORE THE ALTERNATIVES (What choices do you have to help solve this problem?)
- *Hold a joint meeting with teachers and support personnel who can help with this problem*
- *Review key facts and determine what questions need to be answered.*
- *Call the mother to see what questions and information she has that may help the school to help Mark. Consult with the former school if needed.*
- *Talk to Mark about the likes and dislikes of school and what he thinks may help.*
- *Talk to art and computer teacher and ask them to observe Mark's work habits and instructional strategies in their classes.*
- *Observe Mark in various classroom settings.*

ACT ON THE PLAN (Develop a plan, assign responsibilities, and prepare a timeline)
- *Principal—Call Mark's mother to gain insight and explain the process of helping Mark.*
- *Principal and counselor—Form a team of teachers and meet with them. Ask them to keep a learning log of Mark's successes in their classrooms. (When do they occur and what strategies are being used for success?).*
- *Counselor to talk to Mark about experiences at the new school. Help to establish goals with Mark and meet to check over his progress.*
- *Psychologist to observe Mark in various classrooms. Determine the need for testing of Mark.*
- *Assign a teacher mentor to check Mark's classroom progress and a student mentor to help with the transition in the new school.*

LOOK AT THE EFFECTS (how long to implement the plan and when to evaluate).
- *The team will carry out the plan for two weeks and reconvene to discuss progress and changes needed in the plan. Adjustments are made to the plan and efforts are continued.*

IDENTIFY THE PROBLEM

DEFINE THE PROBLEM
(describe the issues)

EXPLORE ALTERNATIVES
(what options do you have)

ACT ON THE PLAN
(develop a plan/timeline for completing the tasks)

LOOK AT THE EFFECTS
(meet and assess the success of the plan)

If the problem is solved to everyone's satisfaction, you may be finished. If the problem has not been resolved, then the cycle must begin again, and a new plan must be developed. Other persons may be consulted to add additional ideas to help resolve the issue.[3]

OUTSIDE THE BOX THINKING
CREATING A PERSONAL MISSION STATEMENT

To help develop consistent behavior as a leader, establish a mission statement for yourself to reflect the culture and climate of your school. Post this mission statement and share it with others. *Follow the guidelines below to help you construct your own Mission Statement.*

What Is a Mission Statement?

A mission statement can be a sentence, a quote, a paragraph, or a page that explains your personal purpose. It is a statement written with much thought and reflection that may change as you mature. It is a description of yourself and your goals for life personally and professionally.

Why Do I Need a Mission Statement?

A mission statement is an important part of defining your personal and professional self. As a leader, you need to understand your own direction in life before you can lead others. A mission statement helps to establish a path for you to maintain your focus and achieve your goals. This statement can remind you of the things that are positive and support your goals as you move through your personal and professional life.

How Do I Write a Mission Statement?

This is an activity that should not be rushed. It requires time for reflection, rewriting, adjustment, and editing. Your statement should be a simple explanation that encompasses the qualities you possess, the direction you wish to take, and the goals you wish to achieve. While this may seem difficult, consulting with people important in your life may help you to develop more insight into what others see in you. When beginning to write, you may want to use these prompts:

- I believe that I am . . .
- In the future, I want to be . . .
- My life goal is to. . . .

You may also gain ideas from looking at persons whom you admire for quotes that support your direction. Such as:

- *"Believe you can and you're halfway there."* ~ *Theodore Roosevelt*[4]~
- *"Spread love everywhere you go. Let no one ever come to you without being happy."* ~ *Mother Teresa*[5]~

What Will I Do with My Mission Statement?

Most mission statements are written for personal reflection, focus, and growth. However, if you are using your mission statement as a guide for yourself in your role as a leader, it can be shared with others on a personal and professional level. This sharing will remind others of what is important to you and where you see yourself moving toward your goal. Posting it in your office or keeping a copy close at hand can also serve as a visible cue for yourself.

Example of a Personal Mission Statement

The first year you become a principal, you should draft a mission statement based on the questions that were included in our directions for Developing a Mission Statement. It may be interesting to look back at those thoughts many years later to see how you have or have not followed them in your personal and professional life. After reading through these, you may discover that you are not far off in understanding yourself and your intended direction in education and your personal life as well. Hopefully, this example may serve to help you in developing a mission statement.

I believe that I am

- a good listener, leader, and teacher;
- a visionary, that I see things as they should be; and
- an "idea" person and that I can inspire others by sharing my ideas.

In the future, I want to be able to

- affect change in children and adults for their betterment;
- teach and lead in a setting where I can influence and inspire others; and
- grow inside and outside my profession through reading, writing, and sharing in personal and professional areas.

My life goals are to be

- able to use my qualities and talents to share with others;
- a child advocate and able to contribute to the wellbeing of children now and in the future;
- sympathetic and helpful to my family and friends; and
- self-reflective and attentive to my own physical, mental, emotional, and spiritual growth.

To promote Inside-the-School Success, the principal should model the process of developing a personal mission statement. The goal would be for everyone involved in the educational process to develop a personal mission statement reflective of the school culture and climate.

MANAGING YOUR STRESS

RATIONALE: Stress manifests itself when your mind and body react to situations that occur for which you may not be prepared. Stress can affect your physical health with symptoms of back and neck aches and stomach distress. Furthermore, stress can cause changes in your personality which can affect your mannerisms and relationships with others. There are many medical remedies available to relieve stress on the job, but these are some strategies used by practicing administrators.

1. Be prepared. See Outside the Box Thinking, *"Organize Yourself and Your Tasks,"* that follows this checklist.

2. Schedule breaks for lunch, walking, and interacting with students and teachers. Take a walk. Get out of the office and walk the halls, the building, the exterior. This helps to provide an avenue for exercise, interactions, supervision, and oversight.
3. Try to accomplish one task at a time. Multitasking can lead to unwanted stress as you are trying to juggle different responsibilities at the same time.
4. Take care of your personal self by scheduling time for relaxation, exercise, family, and visits to the doctor. Get plenty of rest. Make a list of healthy foods that you can eat on the job. Crunchy items such as nuts, or carrots and celery can help to relieve stress.
5. Checklists are a great way to organize. Make them short with two or three items, as your day will be filled with many unexpected tasks. Having a few completed items can give you a sense of accomplishment.
6. Be positive and share positivity with others during your day.
7. Develop a network of peers for collaborating, brainstorming and problem-solving. Identify a "critical friend," or mentor. This person can also be a professor or former colleague.
8. Separate your problems. Feeling like you have many problems and issues can make you feel overwhelmed. Analyze your problems and tackle them separately. Prioritize the most important issues and handle them first.
9. Delegate, delegate, delegate. Rely on persons in key positions to do their jobs. Set expectations and monitor them at scheduled intervals. This will provide you more time for other tasks.
10. Set realistic goals for your day, week, year, to help relieve stress. Review Outside the Box Thinking, *"Establishing Personal and Professional Goals,"* and *"Goal Setting Examples,"* following this checklist.

OUTSIDE THE BOX THINKING
ORGANIZING YOURSELF AND TASKS

Each morning you should review your calendar for the day. It is advised to keep a portfolio calendar as well as an online calendar. Daily, you could write "hot ticket," items on a sticky note and place it on your computer monitor. These would be items that needed to be handled that day. Keep a "to-do list," on your desk and check it each day. Cross out when items are taken care of and rewrite your list on a weekly basis.

As a principal, you should meet every Monday morning with your administrative assistant or team. You should review the calendar for the current week and the following week. By doing this, you will be two weeks ahead with planning and preparation of all the school activities and calendar of events. During this same meeting, for example, if Open House were one of the upcoming activities, you would discuss every detail of what was needed for Open House. Details would include the following: personnel needed, copies of students' schedules, technology equipment needed, rooms/tables availability, and refreshments. This type of preparedness is just as important for summer, opening, and closing of school planning.

Create file folders that can be used with your administrative assistant or other personnel. They can be labeled priority mail, junk mail, and to be signed. These can be placed in your in and out box daily and serve as a great way to keep all documents moving in an efficient and timely manner.

Every Friday morning, you should meet with your Athletic Director or activities coordinator or possibly your secretary and custodian if you are in an elementary or middle school. You should review the sports and/or activity schedule for the weekend and the following week. If needed, you could review coverage for the weekend to ensure that all sports and events are covered. Your Athletic Director or activities coordinator should make you aware of any concerns from opponents or visiting schools, for example, if you were expecting a large crowd that may require multiple administrators to cover sports or events.

You should meet weekly or every two weeks (after school hours) with your administrative team or administrative assistant to review school events, athletic coverage, staff and student concerns, school safety concerns, or overall school concerns. You should also discuss upcoming events and review all the details for the event to ensure that everyone is prepared well ahead of time. *Please note that it is important to conduct these meetings after school hours so that your administrative team or advisors are available during the school day.*

In one of the file drawers of your desk, keep file folders by date of those items that are critical and that you may need to access quickly. There are times in emergency situations where a tangible file folder comes in handy for easy reference. Examples of file folders include:

- School Security Drill—(this would include a write-up of each drill that is held with the exact wording for the PA announcement). This way if you need to do one of these announcements quickly the wording is already prepared during an emergency;
- Teacher contract—Keep all important documents from your teacher's and classified union in this folder for easy access;
- Superintendent (or direct supervisor);
- Administrative or leadership team; and
- Individual students and parents who required more time and attention.

The following suggestions for online organization and efficiency could be used at any grade level. Online folders are helpful for your organization. Some of these titles include: Opening of School, Closing of School, Teacher Evaluations, Classified Evaluations, Awards Programs, Open House, Forms, PTA, and School Security. Create online folders for each one of your administrators and personnel.

To make online communication more efficient, develop several address books. Some examples include a folder for each grade level of students and each grade level of parents in your school. Other online folders could include Department Chairs, Team Leaders, Science teachers, Math teachers, and Coaches and Advisors.

One of the most important organizational tasks would be at the end of each day, clear your desk of all that may have been piled on or taken place that day. Start the next day with a clean desk. As you clear through everything sometimes that is a good way to catch something that you need to take care of before leaving for the day. Plus, you will come to a fresh start on the next day.

OUTSIDE THE BOX THINKING ESTABLISHING PERSONAL AND PROFESSIONAL GOALS

An essential way to deal with stress is to take time for reflective thinking and goal setting. At times, leaders may feel stressed and overwhelmed. Taking time to reflect and set realistic goals can assist with determining the path to achieving personal and professional objectives. Establishing goals is an essential part of leadership and a continuous process involving reflection and assessment. Goals can be long or short term and can guide you through your school day, week, semester, or year. Use the Goal Setting guidelines below to write two to three goals for yourself. Be sure to list steps for achieving these goals and a timeline for completion. See the Goal Setting Example following this topic.

- LONG TERM GOALS—Choose one or two long-term goals you wish to achieve.
- SHORT TERM GOALS—List short steps you will need to complete to reach the long-term goals.
- TIMELINE FOR COMPLETING THE SHORT-TERM GOALS—Establish a realistic length of time you will need to complete each of the short-term goals leading to your long-term goals.
- ASSESSMENT—After a brief period, reflect on your short-term goals and timeline. Ask questions during reflection. *Am I moving to completing my short-term goals? What other goals do I need? Do I need to set new timelines?*

ONCE YOU COMPLETE THE ASSESSMENT, MOVE BACK TO YOUR ORIGINAL GOALS AND MAKE CHANGES. THIS PROCESS IS CONTINUOUS AND REFLECTIVE.

Goal Setting Example

- LONG TERM GOALS—Choose one or two long-term goals you wish to achieve.
    - *I would like to complete my staff evaluations in a timely and efficient manner.*
- SHORT TERM GOALS—List short steps you will need to complete to reach the long-term goals.
    1. *Develop a master calendar of pre-conferences and classroom visits for the persons being evaluated.*
    2. *Create electronic forms to notify staff of pre-conferences, classroom visitations, and post-conferences.*
    3. *Share short-term goals with other administrators for ideas and suggestions.*
    4. *Review the calendar daily to make changes or additions.*
- TIMELINE FOR COMPLETING THE SHORT-TERM GOALS—Establish a realistic length of time you will need to complete each of the short-term goals leading to your long-term goals.
    1. *By September 15th, have the calendar constructed and shared with colleagues.*
    2. *By September 30th, have a rough draft of all needed forms completed.*
    3. *At the first administrative meeting, share forms and calendars with colleagues.*
    4. *Each Monday morning preview the calendar of events to ensure I am on task.*
- ASSESSMENT—After a brief period, reflect on your short-term goals and timeline. Ask questions during reflection. Am I moving to completing my short-term goals? What other goals do I need? Do I need to set new timelines?
    - *Once the calendar was completed and implemented, I realized that changes would randomly occur due to absences, changes in schedules, etc. that would take my time away from the process. At the end of the first grading period, I revised the calendar and forms after seeking input during*

pre-conferences with staff (taking their suggestions into account). I determined that it was necessary to send information both electronically and on paper (using colored forms). I needed to share the calendar with my secretary so that she was aware of my weekly planning and observations. I will continue to review this goal and my procedures at the end of each grading period.

SUMMARY CHAPTER ONE
ONESELF

Developing Personal Traits and Strengths for Inside-the-School Success

Sometimes, when one is in a leadership role, he/she can get lost in the position and forget about the inner self. This section, "Oneself," was designed to focus on the leader within. Looking back at the checklists included, one can find reflective topics. These topics such as Problem Solving, Goal Setting, Mission Statements, Stress, Personal Integrity, and Self-Organization are timely and develop a sound foundation for the demands of the leadership position.

The authors started with this topic because they believe that to have an "Award Winning School," you must start with a well-rounded leader. Time should be spent on developing good reflective practices so that one can rely on this groundwork when the going gets tough. In reading the first chapter, Oneself, the readers should be ready to give thought to the content and determine information valuable to the leadership position in their schools. By completing the last page of the chapter, In School Success, the reader can give thought to the material and select key concepts for practical application. Listed below are some of the key points from Oneself:

- Having consistency in your personal behavior can elicit confidence from your stakeholders.
- Using a problem-solving model can contribute to consistency in your behavior by keeping emotions out of decision-making.
- Effective problem solving is a process that should be studied and practiced.
- The process of developing a personal mission statement should reflect your school culture.
- Writing and sharing your mission statement contributes to self-development as it provides direction for oneself and serves as a visual for your school community.

- Stress affects physical, emotional, and mental well-being. One must develop strategies for dealing with time management, organization, personal care, and collaboration.
- Setting realistic goals for yourself is an essential part of leadership and the entire process contributes to your personal and professional growth.

INSIDE-THE-SCHOOL SUCCESS
READER'S THOUGHTS ON THE CHECKLIST

Reflection is an important part of being a leader. Following your reading, take time to assess the information and consider its meaning and usefulness to you as a principal. Before moving on to the next topic, take time to reflect on the topics you just completed. After reviewing the lists and the supportive materials, choose at least two items and explain how you would use them in your leadership role to ensure school success and Create an Award-Winning School.

_____
_____
_____
_____
_____

Review the *Outside The Box Thinking* included after the checklists or in the appendix to determine how you might use a technique now or in the future in your leadership role. Place your thoughts below on how you may implement this technique or how you might alter the technique to suit your role as a leader.

_____
_____
_____
_____
_____

Be sure to save your thoughts on this topic for future reference.
Try to share something new with a colleague or staff member.

NOTES

1. Bransford, John D. and Barry S. Stein. *Ideal Problem Solver* (New York: Freeman, 1984), 19–41.
2. Bransford and Stein, *Ideal Problem Solver*, 19–41.

3. Bransford and Stein, *Ideal Problem Solver*, 19–41.
4. "Theodore Roosevelt Quotes". BrainyQuote.com, BrainyMedia Inc, 2020. www.brainyquote.com/authors/theodore-roosevelt-quotes, accessed June 2020.
5. "Mother Teresa Quotes". BrainyQuote.com, BrainyMedia Inc, 2020. www.brainyquote.com/authors/mother-teresa-quotes, accessed June 2020.

Chapter 2

Others

Developing Effective People Skills for Inside-the-School Success

As administrators, it is important to develop traits for dealing with the other people that you encounter in your school. The second topic, OTHERS, focuses on principals as they interact with the staff, students, parents, and community members.

This is a relevant topic as it requires the principals to rely on their personal strengths to deal with day-to-day encounters whether positive or negative.

Establishing a healthy organization can help to develop a positive school climate and inviting atmosphere. By placing this topic after ONESELF, the authors are attempting to build upon personal leadership traits while guiding principals into the world around them. Principals become positive models integrating patience, self-discipline, honesty, and integrity along with positive communication skills into their daily interactions with others.

Added to the checklists are "Outside-the-Box Thinking" and narratives to support the topics and provide relevant examples. These can be found after the checklists or in the appendix. At the end of the OTHERS section is an "Inside-the-School Success" sheet for written thoughts by the readers on how they would implement these checklists.

PROMOTING A HEALTHY ORGANIZATION AND A POSITIVE SCHOOL CLIMATE

RATIONALE: A healthy school organization provides an environment in which the players have the capacity to respond to challenges that occur every day. To maintain a wholeness and a healthy learning environment, the principal must provide the leadership. School climate is the atmosphere and the feel of the school that reflects the values and relationships of the persons working and attending that school. A positive climate can be solely responsible for teaching and student learning and success.

1. Create an open environment where honesty and integrity prevail. Be open to suggestions. Construct a suggestion box to gain input from students and staff.
2. Provide accurate, current information to all your stakeholders.
3. Be a supporter of your students. Be visible and approachable. Get to know them.
4. Develop and share a program of positive recognition for your students and staff. Make this a priority for your school as you may impact the entire culture. See *Outside the Box Thinking, Student Positive Recognition, and Staff Positive Recognition* following this checklist.
5. Model behaviors you wish to see in your staff and students. Be aware of your appearance, your verbal and nonverbal cues. Be prepared to deal with Negative People on your staff or in the public. See *Outside the Box Thinking, Dealing with Negative People* following this checklist.
6. Develop high expectations for yourself, your staff, and your students. Share these expectations with others.
7. Be responsive, available, and helpful. Be open to suggestions and criticisms.
8. Encourage proper ownership of problems. Do not assume problems that are not yours but attempt to get the parties together to solve the problems collaboratively
9. Assume the role of a facilitator. Demonstrate to others how to use a problem-solving model to determine alternatives for reaching solutions. See *the IDEAL Model*[1].
10. Develop characteristics of a good problem solvers:

    —Patience—Discipline—Creativity—Openness
    —Honesty—Understanding—Maturity—Tactfulness

OUTSIDE THE BOX THINKING
STUDENT POSITIVE RECOGNITION IDEAS

Student of the Month

To support a positive school climate, it is important to acknowledge student accomplishments in several ways. One example of a program for every school is Student of the Month. Each department or grade level chooses two students per month to be recognized. You should remind teachers to choose those students who may not be recognized otherwise as well as choosing students from various grade levels.

The secretary and principal count the ballots and determine the monthly results. During the first Monday of the month, the principal announces over the PA system the students of the month. The teachers are given an announcement scheduled for the entire school year so they can plan accordingly. The students are asked to report to the office at the end of that class period so that they can be recognized. To recognize the students of the month, the principal can give them a "student of the month," certificate along with a "student of the month school spirited t-shirt." Additionally, each student may have his/her picture taken by the principal's secretary and can be placed on the "student of the month," bulletin board in the common area for all to see.

My Compliments to You! Cards

Another example of recognizing students is by the principal personally handwriting notes and mailing them to students to honor unique accomplishments. See *"My Compliments to You!" cards, Figure A.1, in appendix A*. Some examples of times that you could write and mail these cards could be during homecoming and a holiday program. You should mail a "My Compliments to You!" card to the homecoming queen and king or children in the holiday program. These cards are effective for any grade level of the student.

Following the fall play and spring play and spring musical, you should mail a "My Compliments to You!" card to the student "actors and actresses." Students don't always take the time to say thank you when we support them with their activities, but when we don't acknowledge them or are not visible, they are quick to point it out illustrating how important recognition is.

Positive Referral

It is important that students are called to the office for positive reasons. Teachers can write a referral form for students who have behavioral or academic improvement. See *Positive Referral form, Figure A.2, in appendix A*. The principal or assistant principal could call the students to their office to celebrate their positive referral and call their parent/guardian. A copy of the positive referral form (which is in triplicate) is given to the student, put in the student's file, and mailed home. Positive Referrals could also be used for teachers and staff members.

Spirit Assembly Recognition

As a principal, you could hold three (fall, winter, spring) spirit assemblies per year to promote school pride along with student and teacher recognition. During each assembly, you could recognize both academic and athletic achievements. At the beginning of the assembly, your athletic director or extracurricular coordinator could announce all the athletic teams along with their accomplishments. Following the athletic director's announcement, the principal can announce all the academic accomplishments that took place during that quarter. For example, students earning honor roll, spelling bee or geography bee champion, marching band students who earned honors, or teachers who just finished their master's degrees would be recognized.

The special education and physically handicapped students may enjoy being part of the grade level teams who would compete for the "school spirit award trophy." For example, one competition could be to see which student from each grade level was able to complete the Rubik's cube first.

The physical grade-level competitions during the spirit assemblies to build relationships could consist of games such as hula hoop race, basketball toss, or musical chairs. In order to showcase our musically talented students, we had a grade level "drum off," or "bass guitar challenge," where one student per grade level would compete with each other by playing their drums or bass guitar one at a time. The student body would clap, while our physics teacher used a "sound meter," to detect which student received the loudest applause.

Annual Free Cookout

As a principal, in order to show pride and appreciation, your administration, faculty, and staff could host an "Annual Free Cookout," for the entire student body before a Friday night football game or school event to recognize your students' efforts in being selected as an award-winning school. Your students will enjoy seeing their principal along with teachers, secretaries, and custodians grill their burgers and hot dogs along with the fun conversation. Each year the theme of the "Annual Free Cookout," can change to recognize other student body efforts such as, improving on state-mandated testing, improving on attendance and graduation rates, or reducing incidents of discipline referrals.

Grade Level Academic Award Programs

At the end of each semester or school year, in grades K-8, students could be recognized for academic achievement in subject areas, merit roll, honor roll, and most improved. Your special teachers like art, gym, and music could award students for participation, improvement, community service, and leadership.

As the principal, it is important to recognize students with perfect attendance as well as develop a "Principal's Spotlight Award," in order to recognize students who have been good citizens or for example, who earned their Eagle Scout Award. The Assistant Principal may also have an "Assistant

Principal's Spotlight Award," recognizing students who are good citizens or who have improved behaviorally over the course of the school year.

During the end of the year academic award programs, recognize students per grade level by each department. For example, the English Department or a grade level may choose the top student according to their grades. The awards should always increase in size; for example, first-year perfect attendance award would be a certificate, second-year perfect attendance a small plaque, third-year perfect attendance a larger plaque, and fourth-year perfect attendance a trophy. Varsity academic letters may be given to students for earning three years in a row of a high-grade point average. Varsity academic letters give students who may not be athletically inclined the opportunity to be recognized. Students will be motivated to earn a better award from the year before.

Honor Cords for Graduation or Promotion

In addition to the National Honor Society honor cords worn at graduation, honor cords for both community service and senior projects can be created. For example, if students earn thirty hours or more of community service hours, they qualify for a white community service cord. During eighth grade promotion, students could be given honor cords for academic achievement or community service like builder's club.

Other honor cord examples are seniors who participated in "senior project," the last three weeks of their senior year earn a blue senior project honor cord. Senior project is a program that allows seniors to shadow someone in an area they are interested in pursuing after high school. Community service and senior project honor cords are worn at graduation and give those students who may not be in the top 10% of their class formal recognition.

TEACHER AND STAFF POSITIVE RECOGNITION IDEAS

Teacher and Staff of the Month

Regardless of your grade level configuration in your school, it is important to acknowledge faculty and staff accomplishments in several ways. One example of a program is Teacher/Staff of the month. Students can vote teachers of the month by turning in their voting ballots into the teacher of the month container on the main office counter. Teachers vote staff (secretaries, custodial staff, and cafeteria workers) of the month by turning their ballots into the principal's secretary's mailbox.

The secretary and principal count the ballots to determine the monthly results. During the first Monday of the month, the principal can announce over the PA system the teacher and staff of the month. The teachers can be given an announcement scheduled for the entire school year so they can plan accordingly.

The principal and principal's secretary can visit the teacher of the month's classroom. The principal should announce to the class about the teacher receiving "teacher of the month," followed by a loud applause from the class. The teacher can be given a "teacher of the month," certificate along with a "teacher of the month school spirited t-shirt." The principal's secretary can take a picture of the teacher for the "teacher of the month," bulletin board.

The teacher should fill out a form of their likes and dislikes along with family pictures they would like to share and is posted on the "teacher and staff of the month," bulletin board. The principal and principal's secretary visit the cafeteria or custodian location and present them with the "staff of the month," along with a "staff of the month school spirited t-shirt." The staff member fills out a form of their likes and dislikes along with family pictures they would like to share and is posted on the "teacher and staff of the month," bulletin board. Students enjoy reading new information about teachers and staff members.

My Compliments to You! Cards

Another example of recognizing teachers and staff of the month at each grade level is by the principal personally handwriting "My Compliments to You!" cards and mailing them to teachers and staff to honor unique accomplishments. Some examples of times that a principal could write and mail these cards are as follows: Anytime a teacher organizes a special event or receives community recognition, a card can be sent. During any special event, mail a "My Compliments to You!" card to the teacher who was the advisor and to the custodial staff who had so many additional responsibilities to take care of during this time.

At the end of the classroom observation, you should place a "My Compliments to You!" card on the teacher's desk face down. On this card, you could highlight how organized their classroom was, what a great job they did with positive reinforcement or higher-level questioning skills. Teachers will appreciate this immediate, positive feedback. In fact, teachers might hang their multiple cards from various years on their bulletin board near their desks.

Pizza Lunch with the Principal

One Friday per month for the school year you could provide pizza for the teachers and staff. Always rotate your lunch periods so that different teachers and staff members could attend. This is a great opportunity for teachers and staff members to socialize and to get to know colleagues from different departments. The gesture of "free pizza," is a small way of showing that you appreciate them.

Spirit Assembly Recognition

As a principal, you should hold three (fall, winter, and spring) spirit assemblies per year to promote school pride along with teacher recognition. For example, teachers who just finished their master's degrees could be recognized. Other examples include the following: recognizing a coach or advisor for having a successful season, recognizing a teacher for creating a new program for their students, or volunteering their time in the school community.

Above and beyond Awards

Like the end of the year awards programs you should do for your student body, you could create an "Above and Beyond Awards," program for teachers and staff. The end of the year teacher and staff meeting could be devoted to the "Above and Beyond Awards." These could be awarded to teachers and staff for accomplishments such as club advisors, guidance counselors assisting with state testing, secretaries helping with graduation or special programs, custodians and maintenance crew helping with graduation or promotion, and cafeteria staff helping with refreshments for awards programs.

In addition, each teacher and staff member could nominate others for the "Above and Beyond Award," for accomplishments that deserve recognition and those accomplishments that we may not be aware of. Award recipients would be called to the front of the room to receive their "Above and Beyond Award," certificates while the rest of the group applauded their work.

At the end of the "Above and Beyond Award" program for teachers and staff, you could share a video of teachers and staff who were filmed throughout the school year. Your television and productions studio students could create this video of teachers and staff members doing or saying funny things which can prove to be quite entertaining and is a fun way to end the school year.

OUTSIDE THE BOX THINKING
DEALING WITH NEGATIVE PEOPLE

While stressing the need for positive recognition, it is important to note that not all interactions will be positive. The principalship is a powerful position. You can cast great influence on your stakeholders through your own behavior. The best way to influence most people is to provide accurate, positive information about your school. If people are not informed, then negative information can be used to fill in the blanks. As the principal works to develop a positive school climate, he/she must be prepared to deal with pessimistic or cynical attitudes.

- Be a Good Role Model. Practice being positive in and out of school.
- Think positively. Work at developing a positive schema for yourself. Be open to suggestions and notify others when you have used their suggestions.
- Infect your staff, students, and community members with positive feelings. Greet everyone politely and cheerfully.
- Consider the nonverbal and verbal messages you send. Check your posture and your communications both verbal and nonverbal.
- Identify negative people on your staff. It is important to note who is working with or against the school culture.
- Limit leadership of negative people. Whenever possible, try to limit the influence that they may have on the rest of the positive people.
- Listen to comments from the majority. When most people (who are normally positive) are disgruntled, then it is important to listen to their comments.
- When speaking, refuse to acknowledge negative comments. Maintain your focus and continue speaking. You can always confront that person after you are finished. This might be best addressed later when you can speak to the person privately.
- Avoid contact with negative people unless it is necessary. Only communicate when essential to the operations of your school.
- When necessary, always greet negative people cheerfully, walk away and move on. Maintain your positiveness at all costs. It is essential to the climate of your school.

DEVELOPING SCHOOL-COMMUNITY RELATIONS

Rationale: School-community relations is an area that often gets overlooked in the day-to-day operations of any school. To develop community relations, the principal should make this a planned priority for the entire school. Relationships need to be approved and defined to support the goals of the school and the district, so planning is essential for a successful program. Review these suggestions and implement ones that can enhance your school and community interactions.

1. Develop a committee for the school to include representatives of grade levels, parent groups, support staff, and administration. This committee can be a vital guide for the school's Community Relations program.
2. Establish the goals for community relations for the school. A common goal may be to improve the school program by committing to enhancing learning through positive two-way interactions with community members and groups.

3. Establish a master calendar to note current interactions with the community. Share this information with teachers, parents, and students. Use the calendar as a guide for everyone that may be planning speakers or visitors or who may be planning trips into the community.
4. Establish a system for the screening and registering of visitors and community members. Recognize your supporters by placing photos of their visits and interactions with school members.
5. Provide an In-service session for your faculty and staff. Stress positive interactions with others within the school as well as in the community. The school secretaries are often the first contact with the public and they should be offered continuous training and Inservice.
6. Identify areas in the community for possible field trips that relate to the curriculum.
7. Work with community groups to secure a list of possible speakers for school subjects, historical events, or celebrations. Survey parents as well. They can be a valuable resource for career education, instructional programs, tutoring, and additional materials to support school programs. See *Outside the Box Thinking, Creating a Community School* following this checklist.
8. Challenge each of your teachers and staff to make one connection with a community group, parent, or person to support the school program. One person or group can network with others in the area. Create an "Adopt a Classroom" program so that persons interested in areas of the curriculum or grade levels can support that classroom with financial and personal support throughout the year.
9. Look to the local universities or colleges for community support. There is a wealth of opportunities through college students tutoring, assisting in the classroom, observing, or student teaching. University personnel can also aid in Inservice for your staff, mentoring for your students, and professional growth opportunities for the principal and teachers.
10. Invite school partners to a celebration at the end of the school year so that they can be recognized for their efforts.
11. Evaluate your program. Have the community relations committee take a survey at the end of the school year to gain insight from everyone who participated. Assess the results of your evaluation and how you can make improvements for the future.

OUTSIDE THE BOX THINKING
CREATING A COMMUNITY SCHOOL

An important factor in school-community relations for any school is providing opportunities for the community to come into the school and for the school faculty and students to go out into the community. With much planning, you could create a community school where interaction is a daily part of the school schedule. The community surrounding your school could provide valuable support for your students and teachers. The school can develop into a community within.

So how do you create a community school? Start slowly. Establish goals for your school with your staff. Include support staff also as many live in the community. Assess the needs of your school. Each grade level configuration may have different needs. During the assessment gain input from staff and support staff as well.

The first goal in planning should be for the students and staff to feel and interact like a community within. Meaning that teachers and adults would support each other and that students could support each other as well. This is a task that involves everyone as you brainstorm ways for teachers to help teachers and students help students. Create leadership roles for students such as tutoring programs, safety patrol, hall monitors, cafeteria monitors, office aides, and library assistance. These opportunities provide students with ownership in the school and avenues to help other students. Teachers can find opportunities to help each other through common planning periods, sharing workshop information, team teaching, curriculum support, and mentoring.

Begin by developing small connections that support your program. Starting out the first year, plan for each grade level or subject area to invite a community resource or parents or relatives in to support the curriculum. Guest speakers, career speakers, historians, artists, writers, readers, musicians, and tutors can come throughout the year. Send invitations and thank you notes to the invitees and keep a master calendar so that everyone can observe the interactions.

At the end of the semester evaluate your program to see where changes should be made. You can brainstorm with your committee or have reflective written responses. See *Committee Evaluation Form, Figure A.3, in appendix A*. Some questions that you could brainstorm with your committee concerning internal relationships could be:

- How many connections were made within the school between teachers and staff?
- What connections were made between students in grade levels/subject areas and other students?
- How effective are these new connections (rate them 1–10)?
- Why are these programs effective?

Some questions you could discuss for evaluation of outside community relationships could be:

- What connection/programs have been made between the school and the community?
- Who is involved and when are these occurring?
- Where are these held and how many students and staff are involved?
- How effective are these programs and why?

After the committee evaluates and shares results, it could be time to adjust the program. During the second semester make a goal to find opportunities for students to go out into the community. Chorus or band programs are a sure way to perform for community groups. The staff can compile a list of additional places that could be integrated into the curriculum:

- Seasonal nature walks around the school area;
- Shadow Days for Career Awareness;
- Outdoor education experiences at parks;
- Art Galleries;
- Visiting historical sites or cemeteries; and
- Senior Citizen Homes for reading/performing.

No matter what grade levels are in your school or in what community your school is, there is a place for two-way community involvement. The planning and implementation process is the same.

BECOMING THE INSTRUCTIONAL LEADER

RATIONALE: One of the major roles of a principal is to be the instructional leader for the school. Instructional success involves teachers, students, materials, curriculum, facilities, technology, support personnel, and the principal as the head. At the beginning of your career as an administrator, there are many responsibilities pulling at you, and you need to take time to reflect on your role in the teaching-learning process.

The following list can help you to gain your focus as an instructional leader of the school.

1. Set the tone at the beginning of the year. Know your teachers. Circulate the school when classes are in and out of session. You can learn a great deal by walking the halls, meeting and greeting students and teachers. The more you are out and about, stopping in to see instruction, the more comfortable people will be with you.
2. Become familiar with the state's learning standards in the subjects taught by staff.

3. Sit in on curriculum, team, grade level, or department meetings. Be a listener to understand what the issues of instruction are in your school.
4. Seek input from other administrators when planning observations and evaluations.
5. Be familiar with the teachers' contract and responsibilities for assessment.
6. Take time to develop a calendar for pop-in visits, preconference's, classroom observations, and follow-up conferences.
7. Develop a system of note taking and scripting to keep anecdotal records on instruction.
8. Position teachers as partners. Help set goals for instruction, focus on solutions, and identify resources.
9. Take time to study the teaching-learning process. Become a learner as well as a leader. Know what effective teaching is. Be able to recognize a solid lesson with all the key components. *See Outside the Box Thinking, Effective Teaching* following this checklist.
10. When viewing the classroom, recognize that learning is taking place. Are students responsive, attentive, engaged? Walk around the room observing students as they are learning. Review *Outside the Box Thinking, Engaging the Learner* following this checklist to help identify active learning and to assist teachers in engaging the students.

OUTSIDE THE BOX THINKING
EFFECTIVE TEACHING

As the instructional leader of the school, the principal must be able to assist teachers to improve lesson delivery. The strategies listed below can be shared with staff and implemented in the classroom to improve learning for all students.

- *Develop a Help-Seeking Environment.* Work with your students to be sure that they feel you are approachable and that they can seek help for academics and personal assistance. A positive class climate can help to develop mutual respect for all learners
- *Make Concepts Relevant.* Relate learning to your real-life experiences or to previous student learning. Ask students how they could use this information in real life.
- *Connect Factual Learning with Reading and Writing Daily.* Use logs, journals, records, or prompts to enable students to recreate learning in their own words. Teachers can determine if students understand learning through the reading of written student responses.
- *Break Down Learning into Parts to Improve Memory.* Divide lessons into 15-minute segments. Start with 15 minutes for instruction, 15 minutes of

application, and then 15 minutes for writing, reviewing, and applying the learning.
- *Use Graphics, Diagrams, and Drawings as Visuals to Explain and Reinforce Concepts.* Visuals help to link learning to both sides of the brain. Ask students to draw or develop their own graphic organizers to help with learning.
- *Repeat Key Concepts Regularly.* Formulas, procedures, vocabulary that are the foundations for future learning should be revisited every few weeks. Develop a word wall to post vocabulary throughout the year. Students' journals and logs enable students to write in key concepts and review them on a regular basis.
- *Take Time to Activate Prior Knowledge.* Provide time for students to recall concepts from the past to build on this knowledge. Teacher questioning, brainstorming, and verbal interaction can help students to remember learning.
- *Have Students Teach, Share, and Model Learning for Each Other.* Research has shown that students will retain more information if they teach to someone else.
- *Challenge Students Through the Use of Higher-Level Questions and Written Explanations.* These require more time to answer than standard lower-level problems or simple math computation. Challenging students using problem-solving will help to make them critical thinkers.

OUTSIDE THE BOX THINKING
ENGAGING THE LEARNER

As a principal, one of your major responsibilities is the teaching-learning process. As you observe and evaluate instruction, an important factor is insuring that the learning takes place within the classroom. For students to learn, they must be engaged in the process. As the instructional leader, not only must you observe the teacher, but observe the students as they engage in the process. How can you tell if students are engaged in the learning?

Make instruction a part of the focus of the staff. Include sessions in staff development that focus on engaging the learner to increase knowledge. Have teachers demonstrate the instructional practices that increase learning.

As you visit classrooms, circulate as you observe and note the involvement of the students. The lecture is only one instructional strategy and it creates a passive learner. Look for other techniques that engage the students. *See the Instructional Sandwich diagram figure 2.1.*

Understand that engaged learning is created when the students are the major focus of the instruction. Increasing their interaction with the teacher

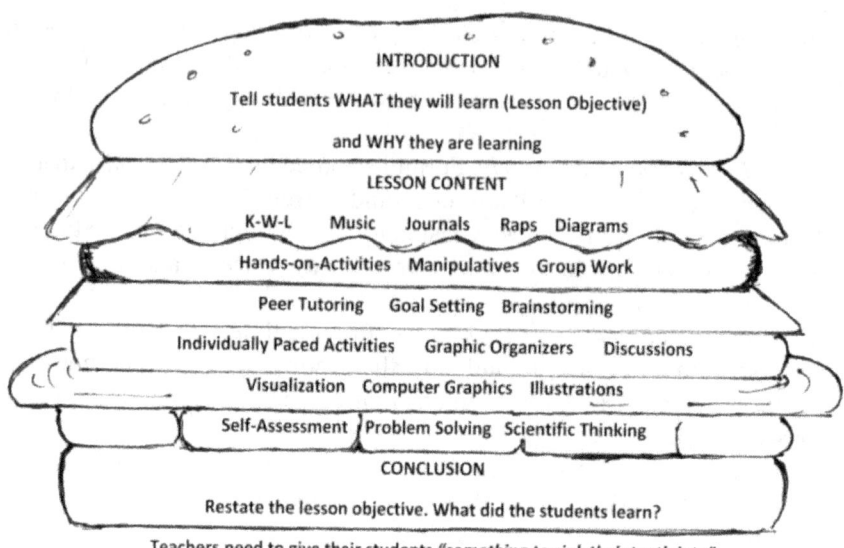

Figure 2.1. The instructional sandwich

and with other students helps to involve them in the lesson and increases responsibility for demonstrating their knowledge.

As a principal, what should you look for? Students working together in cooperative learning groups, together in pairs, or simply being active during the lesson indicates an active learning environment. *Sitting and listening to the teacher is not an example of students assuming responsibility for the learning.*

Develop discussions with teachers on student involvement. Choice in the learning process increases the level of engagement. If students can choose to work alone or with a partner, they may develop more interest in the lesson. Offering a choice in the product is also an option. *Can students submit a drawing, map, or paragraph instead of completing a worksheet to demonstrate their acquisition of knowledge?*

Learning centers or stations can enable the lesson to be broken into smaller components and can include activities to increase the level of engagement of the students. This may be an opportunity to have teachers model for their peers and demonstrate successful use of centers.

Teachers should provide opportunities for students to generate their own work by creating a variety of products to demonstrate learning outcomes. Worksheets, note taking, and copying from the text are lower-level products that require little thought. Deciding how you will demonstrate your own knowledge is a powerful learning tool.

Problem-solving can be integrated into any lesson by posing a higher-level question to challenge thinking. Allowing students time to think about their answers, then sharing their thoughts with each other or with the class can increase interactions and engagement for all the learners.

USING THE INSTRUCTIONAL SANDWICH

The purpose of the Instructional Sandwich (see figure 2.1) is to create a visual comparison with the classroom lesson and its delivery to students. Research has shown that students have better attention and can retain more when they are active learners. The sandwich was developed to serve as an example for teachers that a lesson should have structure and student engagement to enhance the learning experience. The parallel of a complete lesson to a scrumptious sandwich is strengthened by the phrase "*give them something to sink their teeth into.*" While few become satisfied with a simple piece of cheese on bread for a long-lasting sandwich, likewise, students do not learn effectively from a simple teacher-directed or lecture-based lesson in the classroom.

The parallel between the sandwich and the lesson is used to better illustrate the need for introductions, content activities, reflections, conclusions, etc. within the lesson.

Looking at the Instructional Sandwich, the bun illustrates the need for a solid introduction (the top bun) and a solid conclusion (the bottom bun) to hold the lesson (sandwich) together. Each layer of the sandwich includes activities to enhance the lesson and improve student learning. Most people would add layers of meat or vegetables or cheese to their sandwich to enhance its flavor and provide long-lasting satisfaction. Likewise, the teacher should add layers to the lesson to make sure that the students are provided with high levels of engagement and an enhanced learning experience.

The Instructional Sandwich can be a valid tool for principals as they serve in the role of Instructional Leader of their schools. It can be shared with teachers to help to reinforce the need for complete lessons, student engagement, and instructional improvements in the classroom.

IMPROVING COMMUNICATIONS (NONVERBAL AND VERBAL)

RATIONALE: Virtually every leadership function and activity such as planning, decision making, and staffing, can be considered communication.

Effective communication practices involve communicating verbally, nonverbally, and in writing. Valid communication occurs when the message received is close to the message sent and can help to develop a better understanding in the workplace. Since there are many ways to communicate with the school public this topic will define suggestions under each method of communication.

Nonverbal Communication

1. Much can be conveyed to the public through nonverbal cues. The way you stand, facial expressions, hand gestures, arm movement, personal space, and eye contact can influence your message and affect the recipient as well. See *Outside the Box Thinking, Nonverbal Communication* following this checklist.
2. There are also subtle non-verbal cues that can affect the way people perceive your message. Your dress, hair, and overall appearance can greatly affect the observer and intended recipient of your verbal message before it is even given.
3. Other indicators that send nonverbal cues can be the appearance of your office, your desk, your outer office, and the staff you have working for you. The positive climate of your office and your school can promote confidence in you as a leader and can validate your communications.

Verbal Communication

1. Most of your verbal communication will be informal and unplanned. These will be day-to-day interactions with the stakeholders in your building. Because of the casualness of conversation, it is important to think before speaking or answering questions.
2. Try not to be too judgmental or threatening in your approach. When confronting staff or students, speak directly and with feeling. Describe what the person is doing and the effect the person is having. Be specific and explain
3. Accept feedback from people. Be open-minded.
4. Watch your nonverbal cues, posture, expressions, tone, and volume of your voice.
5. Ask questions for clarity. Be specific. Use clear examples to explain your comments. Summarize the conversation so that you understand what has been said.
6. Effective listening is not only hearing but interpreting and understanding the message.
7. Consult *Outside the Box Thinking, Dealing with Irate, Annoyed, and Angry People* following this checklist. Since most of these encounters may be unexpected, it is important to be prepared the details of what you have observed.

OUTSIDE THE BOX THINKING
NONVERBAL COMMUNICATION

One of the important characteristics of school climate is the physical environment of your school which would include office areas, classrooms, hallways, and the school grounds. As a school principal, it is important to keep your office and desk organized and inviting to your school community.

Clearing off your desk before you leave each night, and filing documents where they belong, or getting rid of documents you do not need ultimately reduces stress as you can easily find those important items in a last-minute situation. It is just as important to have current pictures of your students, positive quotes, and education degrees/awards displayed in your office. Student pictures could include sports and activities, pictures of classes, teams, clubs, bands, or organizations. What is important to you such as family and pet photos, and sports you play or enjoy should be displayed in your office.

School community members visiting your office will visibly see your sense of school pride. Displaying positive quotes is a nonverbal way of reinforcing your leadership beliefs and style. Having your education degrees/awards on your office wall reinforces your credibility and experiences.

When members of your school community enter the main office, what message are you sending? Is your main office area inviting, comfortable, and positive? Some ways to have an inviting, comfortable, and positive main office are as follows:

- provide comfortable seating;
- display current copies of your school newsletters (including any literature that positively highlights your school and district);
- to ask visitors if they would like their coat hung up or a cup of coffee/water while they are waiting; and
- display positive quotes and current student pictures displayed.

It is beneficial to form a school climate committee. By forming a committee, it ensures that you have people dedicated to the critical topic of school climate. As a school climate committee, at the end of each school year, you could walk the entire building including classrooms and keep a list of any area that needed improvement when it comes to the physical part of the school climate.

It is essential that your school grounds are kept clean, safe, and inviting. The custodian/maintenance team would make any of the necessary improvements over the summer. This list would include such items as painting in classrooms, bulletin board replacements, student pictures to hang, and murals that art students can paint in a certain area.

Student pictures may include a group of students having fun at a spirit assembly, a teacher demonstrating a physics experiment with their class, or a group of students throwing their caps in the air at graduation. Art teachers could assign their students a school mural to paint as one of their assignments. For example, a mural in the English hallway may be one of William Shakespeare and Emily Dickinson.

In order to cover the costs of nicely framed student pictures, when you sign your school contract with your school picture company, you could ask them if they would include eight free framed school pictures as part of the contract. Since school picture companies are competitive this is usually not a problem as they want to keep your business. Each year, the school picture company could email a folder of all the pictures they took at your various school events, and your school climate committee could choose the eight pictures you want to be printed, framed, and displayed.

Other framed items you could display throughout the school are positive and relevant motivational quotes. For example, quotes regarding the harmful impact of bullying, cyberbullying, texting, and driving, or the importance of nutrition and physical fitness.

Bulletin boards and display cases throughout your school should be up to date. You could assign one of your assistant principals or teachers to oversee all bulletin boards to make sure they are updated per semester. To promote school spirit for each grade level class could have their own bulletin board to decorate each semester. For example, the senior class could include information about prom, graduation, etc. on their bulletin board.

Other school-wide themed bulletin boards could include PTA announcements, Military alumni, Student of the Month, Faculty and Staff of the Month, and Outside of School Activities. It is important to have one "Outside of School Activities Bulletin Board," in order to provide your student body with a place to display information that is non-school related. For example, an upcoming ice-skating competition or Eagle Scouts meeting.

In your school, you could have a courtyard or outside space dedicated to a Memorial Garden. You could have a framed list of all those who lost their lives on 911. You could also have framed pictures of alumni who lost their lives while serving in the armed forces. One of the special education classes could take care of the landscaping of the Memorial Garden by planting beautiful plants and flowers. This landscaping project could serve as one of their life skills requirements. Giving back to your school and community should be a part of the passion of the school and these items support that.

Members of your service clubs could be responsible for fundraising and maintaining the costs of the Memorial Garden. During open house and other community events, the Memorial Garden could be open to the school community.

The sign in front of your school should be updated and used for school events, athletics, activities, and community events. You could assign one of your responsible students the task of updating the sign each week. The student should have access to the school calendar of events.

It's important that all athletics and activities are recognized on the sign; for example, Congratulations to the following Students of the Month, Good Luck to the Cheerleaders in their upcoming competition, Good Luck to Marching Band at States, Congratulations to our National Merit Finalist, and Thank You Voters. When school is not in session, this is a perfect time to publicize important information to your taxpayers about your school and school district.

OUTSIDE THE BOX THINKING
PLANNING VERBAL COMMUNICATIONS

Communications with Small Groups

As a principal, you may have many opportunities to speak to small groups from staff meetings to Parent–Teacher Association, Athletic Council, etc. When you oversee a meeting, it is important to use time wisely as most persons whom you are meeting with are terribly busy and have other responsibilities. Here are some beneficial tips for chairing or participating in a small group situation.

- Always be on time and start the meeting on time.
- Select a location that is convenient to most attendees (i.e. if you are meeting with a department or a grade level, go to their location).
- Provide an agenda, sending it to attendees in advance by email or text.
- Beside each agenda item include a time limit. This will help you to stay on task and signal to others that discussion is limited.
- Have someone other than yourself take notes or minutes to free you to direct the meeting. If you are efficient and can type notes on a laptop, this is a way to combine tasks.
- Establish the purpose and goals for the meeting at the beginning. Reminding everyone why you are meeting and what you plan to accomplish.
- As you review the agenda items, encourage discussion but always be ready to remind attendees of the point of the discussion and the time left to the meeting.
- It can be beneficial to keep a large post-it near you to write down any responsibilities you might have as a result of the meeting. This can be displayed as bullet points and can be referred to after you have returned to your office. The post-it makes it easier to see what it is you must do before the next meeting.

- Try not to waste time by rehashing previously discussed information. It is alright to skip an item if no consensus can be reached during the meeting (table it for further review).
- When you have completed the agenda, review the items discussed and agreed upon. Restate concerns, goals, or additional items that need to be included in the next meeting.
- Verbally thank attendees and follow up with the written notes from the meeting.
- Be sure to be timely in your follow up establishing the next meeting date and purpose.
- Keep your meeting notes and agenda in a binder in a familiar location. Since you may have many meetings to attend, try hanging binders for each meeting. They can be easily grabbed and taken with you.

OUTSIDE THE BOX THINKING
COMMUNICATIONS WITH LARGE GROUPS

Often as an administrator, you may be asked to address a large group on your school program or on district-wide topics. These audiences may know you or may have no information about you prior to the speech. Know your audience. It is helpful to arrive early so that you can speak informally to people and establish some connection. Be sure that you introduce yourself so that they are aware of your position and your knowledge of the subject you are sharing.

- Know your time limits. How long do you have and what is the purpose of your talk? Ask questions about the intended audience. Would they benefit from the use of a PowerPoint or a written handout to take with them? This is essential information for you.
- Be prepared. You should be receiving proper notice of your speech.
- As in the small group meetings, you will want to establish an agenda (with time limits) for yourself and for the persons chairing the meeting so that they are aware of your direction.
- It is advisable to write out items that may have statistics or person names so that you can be correct in the information you share. Typing out your speech may help to stay on task.
- After preparing a speech you can highlight important cues so that you stay on task. Placing your speech, double-spaced, in a binder with sheet protectors, makes it easier to follow. It may be easier to read your speech directly from your iPhone or iPad.
- If you prepare a PowerPoint be sure that there is adequate equipment, lighting, and assistance, etc. Make sure that the PowerPoint is not the dominant force of the speech.

- If you are using a handout, be sure that it is succinct. Limit your shared items to less than ten. Make the print large enough to read and include relevant references in case someone wants to reach you for more information later.
- Once you are prepared, practice giving your speech to check the quality of your voice.
- Remember to look at the entire audience as you speak. Try to be relaxed. To stay on task, keep a watch or timer near you so that you stay within the time allotted.
  - Start with sharing the purpose of your presentation, tell the audience what you are going to do—then do it.
  - Look around at the audience. Walk around a bit as you talk. Share a story or anecdote to gain interest. Break your speech into sections and state what they are—*"I am going to begin by telling you a little history of my school."*
  - When you are done, restate the purpose, thank the audience, and ask for questions.

OUTSIDE THE BOX THINKING
DEALING WITH IRATE, ANNOYED OR ANGRY PEOPLE

In recent times, schools and school personnel have become increasingly aware of the dangers of unwanted visitors or irate parents or community members entering the school. As a principal, most of your encounters should be positive ones. However angry encounters do occur and require different skills. These encounters are often unpleasant and unexpected and may occur after the person has had an unsolved problem with someone else. Knowing in advance how to react to these situations may help to alleviate the "surprise" element of being confronted.

When you are confronted or when you arrive at a scene that is confrontational, take charge of the situation. Move the person(s) to an office or an area of less visibility. Depending on the situation, you may ask a lead teacher or assistant principal to join your meeting as a witness. Let office or safety personnel know that you are meeting with an angry person. Practice these steps before you have an unexpected encounter:

- Speak in a calm unhurried manner and establish eye contact.
- Invite the person to sit down. Listen carefully.
- Maintain your objective while the person vents his/her emotions.
- Keep the discussion focused on the immediate problem.

- Avoid the temptation to respond in a loud, abusive voice.
- Once the person is calm, jot down notes. Paraphrase to show the person you are listening and understanding the message. Clarify misunderstandings.
- WARN the person at any time that you will call the police if the situation becomes threatening to you. Be sure your school safety personnel know that you are in an uncomfortable or dangerous situation.
- Most situations may not be resolved in a short meeting time. Be sure to tell the person that you will respond to them and tell them when to expect your response. Contact them, at that time, even if you have not solved the problem. Let them know you are making progress and trying to resolve the issue.
- Be sure to notify your superintendent or central office personnel about the encounter and seek assistance in solving the problem.
- Buy time. Investigate. Talk to others involved who have more information about the situation.
- Always have a follow-up meeting or phone call. If you are uneasy about meeting the person alone, have someone with you in the meeting.

Keep in mind that persons who are angry over a situation may become angry again at any time. This is an opportunity to red flag a person and share your experiences with others who may have contact with them in the future.

OUTSIDE THE BOX THINKING
PLANNING A WORKSHOP

There may be times when you are asked to share instructional information with your teachers, parents or with fellow administrators, or even a college class. These oral presentations can be daunting, so here are some valuable suggestions on planning instructional large group interactions.

- Determine the length of time of the workshop and the intended audience. Remember even if participants are adults, you can only present 20 minutes of information at a time for the brain to absorb and process.
- Create an agenda for you and the audience. People like to know what you are presenting and what it is you want them to know.
- Establish no more than three goals for the workshop. Decide what it is the audience needs to know.
- Develop a Plan. How will you take the participants from the Known to the Unknown? Be sure to include a strong introduction and conclusion.
- If there is a lot of content, divide it into sections.

- Present a section—then include an activity to engage the audience. Review the materials then connect them to the next section (repeat with activities and review before moving on).
- Develop materials for the audience. Don't read from the handouts, you may even give them after you have presented the section.
- It can also be helpful to present information as a list (i.e. 10 best things to use with children) or (The 7 Cs of Communication). This makes the time organized, keeps you on task, and helps the learner comprehend).
- Develop some reinforcing activities. Depending on the size of the audience, create some 10-minute activities to follow each section of the presentation.
- Note cards are great. List some questions for participants on cards reflecting the content you presented (*i.e. How do you think you could instill safety with your children*). Make groups or partners to discuss the question together then discuss their answers together. You could even list the ideas on the white board, having participants come to the board to write.
- Have the audience develop the conclusion to your presentation. Give them markers and large paper or large index cards. Have them write down one important thing they can take away. Share these, tape to board, etc.
- You can start the presentation by having the audience write questions for you. You can answer them as you go through the presentation or wait until the end and maybe the whole group can contribute to the answers. If you do not know the answers, tell them you will find the answers and email them.
- If you do a PowerPoint, try to discuss the items before you show the screen. You want to avoid having people reading or you reading to them. You also want to avoid having the screen on constantly as people will not talk or will not listen to you.

IMPROVING WRITTEN COMMUNICATIONS

RATIONALE: Effective two-way communication practices should be planned. As a principal, you need to organize your methods of communication and study effective practices. Your plan should include a calendar of dates and scheduled written communications with methods of conveyance. Be sure to focus on how you will communicate in writing to your stakeholders.

1. On your master calendar include dates to in-service the staff on their communications with the public (parent letters, newspaper articles, emails, media releases, etc.). This is essential for continuity in your program.
2. Communication is a cycle involving sending information and receiving information. As a leader, identify your stakeholders. Who are the

publics that need to receive and send information to you? (i.e. Teachers, support staff, parents, students, board members, community groups, and businesses).
3. Plan opportunities for scheduled written communications. People will begin to expect these messages to gain accurate information about the school.
4. Planning written communications involves first determining the following:
   - WHAT is the message?
   - WHO needs to know?
   - WHY does the message need to be conveyed to these persons?
   - WHEN should the message be sent?
   - HOW should the message be delivered?
5. With written communications, you can proofread and think before sending. If you are not good at this task, ask for help. This is an opportunity to be positive. See *Outside the Box Thinking, Planning Written Communications* following this checklist.
6. Determine the method to convey your message. If you use email, Twitter, Facebook, etc. remember that all the messages become the public domain within seconds and can be shared.
7. While informing the stakeholders is important, receiving communications back is just as important to the leader. One must be willing to accept feedback and encourage suggestions and criticism.
8. The most important part of two-way communications is listening and utilizing the comments received. When you are receiving more negative feedback than positive, you need to take these comments into account.
9. When writing an email, newsletter, web page, Facebook entry, etc. remember that most people will scan your document and spend only a few minutes garnering information. It is essential that you use bold type, underlining, color, lists, bullets, and numbering to emphasize the key points you are trying to make. These hints can help to draw in the reader.
10. Consider having a Suggestions Box in your outer office. Develop a card system for writing valid suggestions to you to increase staff input. Include on the suggestion card an area for a conference or personal response if the writer includes his/her name. You may even wish to have help in reviewing suggestions from an assistant principal or counselor in your office.

OUTSIDE THE BOX THINKING
PLANNING WRITTEN COMMUNICATIONS

As a new principal, it is essential to plan your written communications before sending them. Ask someone to proofread especially in more urgent matters when accuracy is critical. Most written communications are not emergencies because the principal would find another avenue to send urgent messages in a timelier manner. As an administrator, it may be necessary to take time to plan newsletters, newspaper articles, letters of importance, memos to the staff, letters of recommendation, etc. A simple chart could help in planning.

WHAT is the message?

WHO needs to know?

WHY does the message need to be sent to these persons?

WHEN should the message be sent?

HOW should the message be delivered?

SUMMARY CHAPTER TWO
OTHERS

Developing Effective People Skills for Inside-the-School Success

The second chapter entitled, OTHERS, was presented to focus on the development of the principal's effective people skills. The role of the principal relies on continuous interactions with staff, students, parents, and community members. Nonverbal communication can send a powerful message to everyone. It is important for leaders to be aware of the methods by which they send nonverbal cues.

Principals must rely on personal attributes to deal with encounters with people, whether positive or negative. Once again, the leader must become a role model and integrate effective communication skills into daily interactions.

- The principal must lead in the promotion of a positive school climate.
- Developing a program of positive recognition for staff and students can impact the environment.
- An important responsibility for the principal is to be the instructional leader of the school. Being visible in the building will help to set the tone at the beginning of the year.
- Observing in the classroom includes the teaching and learning process. It is essential that the principal look for levels of student engagement in the instructional process.
- Effective communication skills include verbal, nonverbal, and written methods. Most verbal interactions are informal and unplanned. However, written, and nonverbal communications should be planned.
- Especially important for a leader is to prepare for unexpected encounters with disgruntled people, whether from the community or within the school. When arriving at a scene that is confrontational, try to take charge of the situation, remain calm and move the person (s) to a safe place for everyone.
- Written communication should be planned and organized. Determining who the stakeholders are that need to receive the written message, will help to determine the best method by which to communicate.

INSIDE-THE-SCHOOL SUCCESS
READER'S THOUGHTS ON THE CHECKLISTS

Reflection is an important part of being a leader. Following your reading, take time to assess the information and consider its meaning and usefulness to you as a principal. Before moving on to the next topic, take time to think about the topics you just completed. After reviewing the lists and the supportive materials, choose at least two items and explain how you would use this information in your leadership role to ensure school success and create an Award-Winning School.

_____
_____
_____
_____
_____

Review the *Outside the Box Thinking* included after the checklist or in the appendix to determine how you might use a technique now or in the future in your leadership role. Place your thoughts below on how you may implement this technique or how you might alter the technique to suit your role as a leader.

_____
_____
_____
_____
_____

Be sure to save your comments on this topic for future reference. Try to share something new with a colleague or staff member.

NOTE

1. Bransford and Stein, *Ideal Problem Solver* (New York: Freeman, 1984), 19–41.

Chapter 3

Organization

Developing Systems and Schedules for Inside-the-School-Success

Effective organizational skills are a key for administrators. It is essential to demonstrate time management, planning, communication, problem-solving, and team-building skills for a successful organization. This topic, ORGANIZATION, is the cornerstone for successful operations in the school.

Included in this topic are:

- preparations for the school year;
- strategies for scheduling at all grade levels;
- guidelines for student management and discipline; and
- hints for organizing athletics and extracurricular activities.

This is a relevant topic as it requires the principal to develop the consistent skills needed to lead staff in collaborative efforts. The organization of schedules, students, and events will lead to the improvement of the overall operations of the school. The authors provide support for the topics through narrative reflections and essential charts and forms from their own experiences.

GETTING READY FOR SCHOOL

RATIONALE: As a principal, it is important to get the school year off and running smoothly. In the first month of school, how well everything goes can set the tone in your building either positively or negatively. In order to have a smooth opening of the school year it is important to do the following ahead of time: Communicate to all stakeholders, create well-organized orientation programs for students and new staff, and ensure that materials and your building are ready. See *Beginning of School Checklist Figure B.1, in appendix B.*

The following list can help you have a smooth opening of the school year:

1. Before the school year begins, meet with your summer staff to organize a final building check. The building should be clean and ready for the first day. See *Facilities Walk Through Checklist, Figure B.2, in appendix B.*
   - The Code of Conduct should be posted throughout the building.
   - Emergency instructions (Fire, Tornado, etc.) should also be posted.
   - Clocks, bells, classroom furniture, and lockers should all be inspected and repaired.
   - Locks for lockers (if applicable) should be inspected, and combinations changed.
   - All hallway bulletin boards for athletics and activities need to be updated.
2. Double check that all new hires have been completed. This would include both certified and classified staff.
3. Review and create the school-year calendar with your secretary and administrative team. At the middle and secondary level, divide extracurricular activities or club supervision amongst your administrative team or supervisory staff for the fall semester.
4. Check with office staff and curriculum coordinators to make sure that all textbooks, supplies, and materials have been received. All technology should be earmarked for cleaning and repairs.
5. Be sure to have all forms printed and stacked for teacher distribution. This includes class lists and study hall lists. Student Handbooks/Planners need to be printed and ready to distribute.
6. Homerooms and classrooms should be assigned. Schedules should be finalized, printed, separated by homeroom, and ready to post or distribute.
7. Teacher manuals need to be updated online and a list of any changes should be created to share with teachers.
8. Staff mailboxes and substitute folders should be set up and ready for review. School and classroom keys should be checked and distributed ready for teachers/staff.
9. Plan entry grade (Kindergarten, Sixth, or Ninth) Grade Orientation. Be sure to include PTA, guidance staff, teachers, athletic director, coaches, and advisors. Advertise the date of the program with local media sources. Organize informational tables in your cafeteria with athletic, and extracurricular and after-school programs. Create a meeting agenda and have schedules and lockers ready where applicable.
10. Create and send the principal's letter to the staff and the principal's newsletter to parents and students.

11. Prepare teacher and staff first-day agenda and new teacher orientation, see *Faculty Meeting Sample Agenda, Figure B.3, in appendix B.*
12. Prepare the first week of school for students including class meetings. Make sure that your administrative team and staff are highly visible and available especially during the first month of the school year.
13. As part of your teacher's opening of the school year packet, see *The Administrative Responsibilities Chart, Figure B.4, in appendix B.* This chart is an efficient way for your teachers to know which administrator to turn to as they navigate the school year. This same chart can be adjusted with other administrative team personnel for use at various grade levels.

OUTSIDE THE BOX THINKING
PREPARING FOR SCHOOL

The process of preparing for a new school year is not just a summer task for the principal. It is a year-long continuous effort by the leader and the entire staff. Preparations for the next school year should begin as the current year unfolds. As meetings and classes are held and personnel are in place, the principal should analyze issues and concerns and begin to take note of the processes and operations that have been effective or ineffective. This should be an all-encompassing task with input from everyone.

At the onset of the year, the principal should develop a system to gain suggestions and concerns from the stakeholders. Using committees that are in place within the school (teacher and student advisory councils, administrative teams, etc.), the principal should begin to encourage and gain input. A suggestion would be to begin by developing a notebook, or online folder, or a visible chart of issues and needed changes for the future. This would provide everyone with a visual of the leader's plans.

In addition, a thorough evaluation should occur after the first term of school. This could include:

- enrollment predictions;
- curriculum changes;
- materials request;
- facilities updates;
- needs for additional staff; and
- building and district financial concerns.

While this would assist in planning for the closing of the year, it could be a vital part of the plans for the next year as well. It is essential that time be allotted for guided reflection by the staff with the principal. This joint planning will ensure that everyone has had input in the conversation.

As the second semester evolves and the summer approaches the school leader is often occupied with finalizing procedures and preparing the exiting students and teachers for departure. There is a clamor to get books, tests, computers, grades, rooms, and materials counted and prepared for closure. Taking time to reflect as a staff on the results of the planning process that the leader began earlier in the year, will help to guide the closing of school, and prepare for the next year.

So much work is completed to close the school, that the principal should not lose focus on the future and the next school year. It is apparent for the principal, that as the year evolves the focus is on the present, while examining the past, but planning for the future.

THE MOST EFFECTIVE WAYS TO HANDLE STUDENT DISCIPLINE

RATIONALE: While school discipline may differ between grade levels and schools, many factors are consistent and should be handled using similar procedures and practices. Some K-8 schools will have the principal handle the discipline issues. The assistant principal at the high school level may handle student management, whereas the principal may handle adult management. However, the high school principal will normally get involved with more serious student discipline issues. Student discipline issues need to be handled in a fair, consistent, and *timely manner* (24–48 hours unless it is a serious offense that needs to be handled immediately).

When schools have more than one administrator managing student discipline, it is important to be fair and consistent so that everyone is on the same page. See *Discipline Consequences Grid, Figure B.5, in appendix B*. No matter what grade levels are in your school, it is important to note that how student management is handled can have a critical impact on the overall school climate and learning environment.

1. Begin by having teachers develop and post classroom rules and consequences. See *Classroom Discipline Plan, Figure B.6, in appendix B*. This plan should be on file with the office to ensure continuity within the school. At the secondary level, you might require detailed guidelines of classroom expectations including syllabus and grading policies. See *The Classroom Management Plan Assessment, Figure B.7, in appendix B*.
2. Create a discipline grid of consequences with your teachers or administrative team, like the one provided, that correlates with your current

student discipline issues. Make sure that everyone responsible for student discipline is following the agreed-upon discipline grid. When using this discipline grid, there may be extenuating circumstances like special education or environmental factors that may require flexibility.
3. Update your student code of conduct/handbook prior to the beginning of the school year for board approval. Be sure to add any new discipline situations that may have taken place the previous year. Keep a list of new incidents throughout the school year so that they can be easily added to the student code of conduct.
4. Order and update all forms that pertain to student management. It is important to be organized and have a system of handling the paperwork that comes with student discipline. See *Discipline Incident Report, Figure B.8, in appendix B*.
5. Conduct grade-level meetings to review school rules and the student code of conduct within the first five days of school. Create a PowerPoint that not only explains the rules but why the rules are in place. Provide a copy of the code of conduct for all students and parents to sign. Create a report to be sure that all have signed and understood the student code of conduct.
6. Remember to share a positive referral system with your students so they know there are ways they can be recognized for positive behavior. See *Principal's Good News Calls, Figure B.9, in appendix B*. This system involves teachers and staff in nominating students for calls made by the principal.
7. When disciplining students, keep your own records including names, teachers referring, infractions, anecdotal notes, persons called, messages left, etc. This information is important for data analysis and appeal hearings.
8. Create an Intervention Assistance Team[1] or a committee to help with at-risk students. Analyze your data to help you determine for example if the same teacher is writing referrals? At what locations and times are the incidents occurring? How can you help this student? See *Outside the Box Thinking, Developing Programs for Discipline Interventions* that follow this checklist.
9. Discipline data can result in the following:

- Assisting a teacher with student management who is writing several referrals.
- Increasing visibility where incidents are continuing to occur.
- Conducting student behavior contract meetings with counselors, parents, and administrators for those repeat offenders.
- Administrators for those repeat offenders.
- Reviewing consequences for incidents that continue to occur.

10. Be proactive and not reactive. Students are less likely to cause discipline issues if they know they have someone to turn to. Administrator and staff visibility can help deter problems. Create a "duty schedule," for your administrative team and staff members including lunch hours, between classes, and before and after school. Build rapport with your students. *Students do not care what you know unless they know that you care.*

OUTSIDE THE BOX THINKING

How to Use the Discipline Consequences Grid (Figure B.5)

When you have multiple administrators overseeing student management, it is important to be consistent. In a large school, administrators are usually assigned to a particular grade level of students and move with the class until they graduate. To avoid complaints that students in the other classes are not receiving the same discipline consequence for the same offense, it is important to adhere to the code of conduct. Part of the problem happens when the consequences for certain student behavior are not easily spelled out and are left up to each individual administrator.

Could this system be used at other grade levels? It is certain that middle and intermediate grades could benefit from a similar system of organizing behaviors, particularly if in a larger school population. In the primary grades, a principal may want to develop a system on a smaller scale. This could really help if there is an assistant principal involved in disciplining students as well. A less complex grid could assist administrators in developing some consistency in the disposition of discipline issues.

Therefore, you should work together with your administrative team to create a Discipline Consequences Grid. By having each administrator on your team adhere to your Discipline Consequences Grid it ensures fair and consistent treatment for each student. For example, whether you are a freshman or a senior if you have been tardy to school three times, your consequences will be the same. Each summer you should edit the Discipline Consequences Grid by adding new offenses or adjusting consequences depending on the need of your school and the students you are working with.

The different abbreviations within the Discipline Consequences Grid are as follows:

- *ISACP* stands for In School Alternative Classroom Placement. You may be familiar with In School Restriction. They are one and the same. Students are placed in an alternative classroom while they work on classwork and

receive credit for all classwork completed. The ISACP can be monitored by various teachers or paraprofessionals.
- *OPS* stands for Opportunity School. Opportunity School was held on Fridays after school for one hour. You may want to choose Fridays as that is the day students are usually excited to start their weekend. This is the student's "Opportunity," to change their behavior before receiving a Saturday School. Students are required to work on homework during this time. Opportunity School can be monitored by the same teacher as a supplemental. Saturday School is held for three hours on Saturday morning, monitored by the same teacher as an annual supplemental.
- *OSS* stands for Out of School Suspension. The first time a student receives an OSS for the school year, they can make up all schoolwork and receive credit. The second time and all subsequent OSS the student receives a zero for all schoolwork missed including quizzes and tests.
- Noted on the Discipline Consequences Grid as first, second, third, and so on, for example, stands for the 1st time the student is tardy to school, the 2nd time the student is tardy to school. The items on the right column are the consequence. N/A means no consequence, just a verbal warning, and discussion with the student as to why they should change their behavior. "Administrative Discretion," means just that, it is up to the administrator as to what the consequence will be. With minor discipline behaviors, the administrator may choose to give a warning whereas with more serious discipline behaviors the administrator would discuss with the administrative team as to what a fair consequence would be. For example, "sexual harassment," can cover a large spectrum of behaviors, therefore, a discussion with the administrative team is needed to decide on fair consequences.

What is the result of utilizing the Discipline Consequences Grid? Your students know that your student management is firm, fair, and consistent. By following the Discipline Consequences Grid consistently, when students come into your office for consequences, they know the outcome ahead of time because it is that consistent.

The level of consequences within the Discipline Consequences Grid also sends a message to your student body. For example, if they swear directly at a teacher or choose to assault someone, they receive serious consequences. This really helps to reduce incidents of serious discipline behaviors by your students. Increasing the seriousness of the discipline consequence for repeated behavior communicates to your student body and parents that you are giving your students the opportunity to change their behavior way before the consequence becomes more serious. However, serious discipline behaviors require serious consequences from the beginning.

Depending on the student management issues you are dealing with at your school you can also take away privileges along with the discipline consequences. For example, beginning in January, you could announce that anyone suspended for drugs or fighting will not be allowed to attend Prom. In reverse, you could announce anyone who has not been suspended since January will receive $10.00 off the cost of their Prom ticket.

Another example is the use of cell phones. Every educator complains about the headaches of the inappropriate use of cell phones by their student body. You could allow students to use their cell phones before the start of the academic day, after the end of the academic day, and during their lunch period. You could provide an individual storage location in every classroom for students to drop off their cell phones. You could also implement a Bring Your Own Device (BYOD) and allow students to utilize their cell phones in class or during class assemblies for educational or planning purposes at the approval of their teacher or administrator.

By providing designated time for students to use their cell phones, it makes the argument that much easier when you must take their cell phones away for inappropriate use. The first time their cell phone is misused you would give it back to them at the end of the school day. The second time their cell phone is misused, their parent/guardian must pick it up. By involving parents in this process, it really reduced the number of cell phone incidents. Parents will be supportive since you are allowing cell phone privileges throughout the day.

Using the Discipline Consequence Grid as a school administrator can decrease inappropriate behavior over time. The consistent use of the Discipline Consequence Grid, as well as positive reinforcement programs, can significantly reduce your incidents of violence. In most instances, teachers will appreciate the consistency of student management by their administrative team and know they would be supported when they wrote a discipline referral.

OUTSIDE THE BOX THINKING

Classroom Management Plan Assessment (Figure B.7)

As a principal, structures and forms can be created as a need arises. An example of such a form is the Classroom Management Plan Assessment. Parents' and students' concerns can be eliminated by having each teacher include every item listed on their Classroom Management Plan Assessment on their course syllabus. Most importantly parents and students have a clear understanding of every class of their teacher's expectations.

In other grade levels, it is a necessity to have all teachers coordinate their classroom discipline plans with the school-wide rules and consequences.

Having a written plan that is shared, posted, and stored in the office can provide uniformity and accountability. Some grade levels can write plans together particularly in the middle grades. Using the sample Classroom Management Plan Assessment can help to provide structure to school discipline as well as integrate positive consequences.

It is important to add a disclaimer stating, "This is not meant to be all encompassing. As the year progresses, there may be a need for additional assignments or modifications or expectations." In the cases where a teacher needs to add an assignment; for example, an additional powerpoint presentation, parents could not say their student was not going to do it because it was not on the original syllabus.

During teacher check out, on the last day of the school year, each teacher should be required to hand in their syllabi for the upcoming school year along with a copy of the Classroom Management Plan Assessment. If needed, you may want to assign teachers alphabetically amongst your administrative team so that each administrator has a percent of the Classroom Management Plan Assessments to evaluate. The administrator(s) should be required to return the Classroom Management Plan Assessments to their teacher's mailbox before leaving for the summer. This allows teachers to make corrections needed and copies for their students prior to the start of the school year.

The overall practice of requiring a Classroom Management Plan Assessment allows for transparency amongst administrators, teachers, students, and parents when it comes to classroom expectations and consequences. In addition, when working with a new teacher you should have examples of the excellent syllabi to share with them.

OUTSIDE THE BOX THINKING
DEVELOPING PROGRAMS
FOR DISCIPLINE INTERVENTION

The best way to manage discipline as an administrator is to be proactive by knowing who the at-risk students are and providing them with the services, they need to prevent discipline issues. When students transition from one building to another or middle school to high school, personnel should try to ensure that the incoming school is aware of all the students who are on an IEP (Individualized Educational Plan) or 504 plans. It is just as important that the incoming school administration and staff are made aware of at-risk students who are not on an IEP or 504 but who have been a discipline problem at their previous school.

Before students enter middle or high school, it is important to coordinate a meeting between the high school administrative and counseling team along with the middle school administrative and counseling team to review all incoming ninth graders who are considered at-risk but are not on an IEP or 504. For example, if one of the incoming ninth graders were in trouble a lot for bullying, the team could collectively determine the reasons for the behavior and what the interventions would be.

The intervention for this student may be to schedule the student with teachers who have a more nurturing teaching style. The guidance counselor could do a weekly check-in to monitor how the student is doing emotionally and academically. In addition, you could make this student an office assistant during their study hall so that as the principal you would have daily interaction with the student and could monitor their mood and ask them how they are doing.

At lower grade levels, it is also important for the administrator to lead interventions for students having behavioral or discipline issues. It is essential to implement an Intervention Assistance Team (IAT). This team consists of counselors, teachers, principals, and supportive personnel. Together you should analyze and research students' problems, make observations, and recommendations for interventions. See *Outside the Box Thinking, Implementing Intervention Assistance Teams for Any Grade Level* that follows this section.

One advantage of an IAT is that thorough written records are kept on students that could be shared with parents, future teachers, and administrators in other buildings. The best advantage is that professionals come together to analyze discipline and brainstorm valid solutions to assist students to have successful school experiences.

Discipline is a task that is best addressed by including all staff, parents, and students to help in tackling issues and providing opportunities for growth.

Freshman Transition Program

Professional Learning Community (PLC) model by Richard and Rebecca DuFour and Robert Eaker (June 2004)[2] is a successful way to structure your school. It is invaluable to be trained in the PLC model. Under the PLC model, there are building goal committees that create a school-wide system of interventions by providing all students with a variety of support systems. Just like special education students receive intervention and assistance, at-risk students academically or behaviorally receive additional support.

The administrative and counseling teams can create a "Freshman Transition Program," which is part of the PLC model which was designed to assist students who may have had a history of achieving below their academic potential. These students may not show much interest in school and/or may need help with time management, note-taking, test-taking, study skills, reading comprehension, communication skills, and listening skills.

During the summer, you should send a letter to the parents of incoming freshmen who are considered at-risk explaining your Freshman Transition Program. You should explain to the parents that to give their son or daughter every opportunity to succeed at your high school they should enroll their student in the Freshman Transition Program. The Freshman Transition Program should be part of your high school curriculum and offered during the school year for one daily class period. If parents are interested, they could fill out a registration or call the ninth Grade Assistant Principal or Guidance Counselor should they have further questions regarding the program.

A teacher who volunteers should teach the Freshman Transition Program class. This is included as part of the teacher's total class load with time to plan and organize. The teacher should do a daily check in on the student's homework assignments and make sure the students are completing them accurately. In addition, the teacher should check their grades in all their classes weekly. Outside guest speakers could be invited to speak on topics such as: career choices, college readiness, and organization strategies. Teachers, counselors, and administrators could speak to the class on topics to help them be more successful.

Research has shown that students involved in this program increased their GPA. It is important to build a reward system by recognizing students who improve throughout the year.

This program has a great deal of value and can serve as a model for other grade levels at other schools. Early identification and intervention for students who are academically or behaviorally at risk at middle and elementary schools can lead to success for these students.

Mentor Program for Seniors (or Other Grade Levels)

As part of following the Professional Learning Community (PLC)[3] model of providing intervention programs for all students, a Senior Mentor Program should be created. *Please note that this mentor program could be implemented at various grade levels using teachers, support staff and parents as mentors.* Seniors get distracted with all their senior events (also known as "Senioritis") so you may want to have each senior mentored to keep them on track for graduation. The Senior Mentor Program helps seniors be more successful and improves the overall graduation rate.

Your senior guidance counselor should provide an alphabetical list in a binder of every senior. Administrators, guidance counselors, teachers, and staff members which included school secretaries serve as mentors and could choose at least five seniors to mentor for the school year. Secretarial staff members enjoy being part of the Senior Mentor Program. It is important that mentors choose seniors that they already had a relationship with or thought they would be able to connect with.

Mentors should meet with their five senior mentees once per week or a minimum of twice per month depending on the needs of their seniors. During these meetings, discussion topics would include, for example, grades, questions regarding senior-related items, the stress of the college application process and acceptance, family issues, and who they wanted to go to prom with.

As the principal, you too could choose five seniors to mentor for the school year. The weekly meetings with the seniors you mentor are extremely helpful for them as they transition through their senior year. Since every senior has a mentor this program not only includes at-risk seniors but your seniors with 4.0 plus grade point averages as well. These seniors appreciate having a mentor to discuss topics such as the stress they were feeling regarding the college acceptance process or trying to get into an ivy league school.

OUTSIDE THE BOX THINKING
IMPLEMENTING INTERVENTION ASSISTANCE
TEAMS FOR ANY GRADE LEVEL

Within your school, students may struggle *academically, behaviorally, or emotionally* and may not receive the interventions needed to be successful. Often students must be identified for special programs to receive services to assist them to achieve at school. For any principal, no matter what grade levels they have within their school, a solid suggestion is to implement an Intervention Assistance Team (IAT).[4] These teams are sometimes referred to as Teacher Assistance Teams or Student Intervention Teams. No matter what the title, the purpose of this team is to identify and intervene to benefit students through a process of systematic problem-solving.

Regardless of the grade level of students, these teams can provide powerful support for teachers and for students and parents as well. Many schools combine the workings of an IAT with a Response to Intervention (RTI)[5] Team. Both teams examine data and implement problem-solving strategies and suggestions for positive student interventions. The difference between these formats is that the IAT relies on teacher referral and can be for academic, social, emotional, or behavioral reasons. The RTI usually focuses on academic assessment and instructional intervention as early as possible to benefit the struggling student.

The fundamentals of an IAT are for the principal to form a team of experts (psychologists, special education teachers, and counselors) that are available in the school. Sometimes in an elementary school, lead teachers can become experts in interventions strategies and substitute for other positions that might not be available. The principal, as an instructional leader, should serve as the chair and form a standing committee of professionals and interested persons. The focus is on shared decision-making and problem-solving. Classroom teacher involvement includes identification of students, referral to the IAT, preparation of materials for the team, and serving as an active member of the problem-solving experience.

The main goal is for the team to provide a plan to assist classroom teachers in analyzing student problems and identifying the source of the problems. Along with the teacher, team members aid in developing techniques that can be successful for the student. The process is one that involves the completion of research, observations, and acquisition of information about the student. The meetings are organized, and formal and additional resource persons may be invited to attend.

Because the IAT can provide a thorough expert analysis of the student, in some schools, a referral to the IAT may be required before a student is considered for special education testing and services. Results of the team investigation may provide significant resolve to student issues that may have required psychological testing or special class placement.

How to Begin:

- As the principal, share ideas with the experts available to the school, such as counselors, special education teachers and psychologist, speech therapists, etc. Forming a core group will help with organization, structure, and communications. All members should receive training before beginning the process.
- Establish a standard meeting date and time so that all members know in advance. Develop a calendar so that referring teachers are aware of your meetings.
- Develop forms for teachers to use for referral and for minutes to be recorded and later shared with all participants.
- Teachers' referral forms are shared with all committee persons prior to the actual meetings.
- Form a standard agenda with strategies and time limits to keep the meetings on task. Suggestions might be:

  — The referring teacher explains problems and shares data collected. 10 minutes
  — Committee members ask questions. 10 minutes.
  — Committee and teacher brainstorm strategies that might be implemented. 5 minutes
  — The committee develops a plan and assigns person's duties. 5 minutes
  — The chairperson reviews the plan and sets the follow-up meeting. 5 minutes
  — The next meeting time should allow everyone involved to complete the given tasks in a timely manner.

- Everyone who attended the meeting is sent a copy of the plan and timelines to finish the strategies. (*An example might be the psychologist will complete an observation during the student's art class by October 3*).
- The principal should remind everyone to be prepared to share their findings during the follow-up meeting. The principal is the instructional leader and can contribute a lot of valuable information to both the IAT and RTI teams. These are both essential components for a school to assess and intervene for the benefit of the struggling student.

CREATING THE MASTER SCHEDULE K-12

RATIONALE: An essential part of the principal's duties is to ensure that the master schedule is completed in a timely and effective manner as it impacts both students, teachers, and daily operations. Scheduling requires a team of experts and staff members knowledgeable about curriculum and instruction. When available, it is important to have your administrative and guidance staff as part of your master schedule team. While creating your master schedule, it is important to create one that is student driven. *While scheduling practices differ from grade level to school, basic concepts apply to all principals and will be shared at the beginning of this checklist.*

1. If you are new or have hired a new administrator or guidance counselor, send them to a master schedule training conference through the summer or at the beginning of the school year so that they are properly prepared on how to build a school master schedule.
2. Study the current schedule and interview teachers on projected needs and current existing problems in the schedule.
3. Check your grade level enrollments and your current class loads. Be aware of the needs of your special education teachers and students. Classroom inclusion involves a great deal of planning and should be a priority.
4. At the beginning of each school year, develop guidelines for creating a master schedule. See *Guidelines for Creating a Master Schedule, Figure B.10, in appendix B*. This chart should include the following: tasks that need to be completed, duration of each task, date to begin and complete each task, along with the person(s) responsible for tasks.
5. Create your team to assist you in scheduling. Meet with them earlier and share your timeline and scheduling process. Your role on this team may change between school districts or between grade level configurations.

At the elementary, you may be the only person involved but in the middle school, you may assume the role of advisor.
6. Check with the central office on budgeting needs for projected new course offerings or the addition of classes due to projected enrollments.
7. Plan a calendar to include dates for completion of the master schedule, student meetings, course selection sheets, and orientations for incoming students (eighth grade for high school, fifth grade for middle school, and kindergarten for elementary school).
8. Advertise and plan for incoming students, including from private schools and community preschools (if elementary level).
9. Communicate with staff before the end of the school year to share proposed schedules, enrollment, room assignments, and equipment needs.
10. Understand that changes may have to be made through the summer or right before school starts. Rely on the members of your scheduling committee for support and advice throughout the process.

PLANNING THE HIGH SCHOOL SCHEDULE

RATIONALE: As an administrator at the secondary level, one must understand the process for scheduling. While the principal may not be directing the operations, the ultimate responsibility for the completion and implementation of the schedule relies on the administrative team. The master schedule chart applies to all students which includes: Career Tech, Post-Secondary Education Options, and online students. The following list explains the tasks to create a master schedule in more detail:

1. Department chairs should submit all new course proposals by mid-September of the year preceding the new scheduling. New courses will be added to the program of studies for the following school year. It would be important to create a standard course proposal form for all your departments.
2. Review new course proposals and seek board approval for all new courses.
3. Department chairs should submit all program of studies revisions by mid-October. Administrative and guidance staff review program of study changes.
4. Program of studies should be edited, printed, and placed online by mid-November.
5. Course selection sheets should be developed and printed. New course requirements mandated by the state as well as newly created courses should be edited. Administrative and guidance staff should review updated course selection sheets by January of the year preceding the implementation.

6. Incoming freshmen and parents should be invited to orientation by mid-January. Remember to invite parents from the surrounding parochial schools. Administrative and guidance staff should organize the agenda and presentations explaining high school course requirements and offerings. After the program, parents should meet with department chairs and ask content-specific questions. Each department chair should have a table setup displaying textbooks.
7. By mid-January, administrative and guidance staff should visit the middle school(s) and share the same presentation that was shown at a parent night to the current eighth graders. This same presentation can be shared with surrounding parochial schools.
8. Guidance staff should begin scheduling with current eighth graders in early February. This is followed a few days later with a recommendation day and course selections sheets filled out by current eighth graders.
9. By mid-February Guidance staff should host scheduling meetings for ninth—eleventh graders. High school course recommendation day should take place by the third week of February. The guidance staff should review and enter all course requests (including current eighth graders) by the beginning of March.
10. The administrative and guidance staff should work together to develop course needs from the student request data by mid-March.
11. The administrative team will finalize the high school teaching staff needs based on course request data. The principal must meet with the superintendent to obtain final approval of staffing needs.
12. Prior to finalizing the schedule, department chairs should give input to the master schedule team on teaching assignments. Each teacher will need to fill out a teaching assignment sheet that lists preferred classes they would like to teach along with their teaching certification. This is important information to have while you are building the master schedule. *(See Teaching Assignment Sheet, Figure B.11, in appendix B)*.
13. Once all parties have had an opportunity to give input, the team will create the master schedule. For the process, two full days should be allowed without interruptions. Blocking out a Friday and a Saturday by the end of March can help to ensure the work gets completed.
14. The master schedule team should follow by inputting the master schedule and running simulations.
15. You should provide a draft of the master schedule to department chairs for input by the beginning of May.
16. Teachers may be given a tentative teaching assignment by the end of May.
17. The master schedule team should continue to work on remaining scheduling problems, creating and mass adding study halls, and lab study halls by the end of June.

18. Finally, the master schedule team inputs and updates the final draft of the master schedule and distributes it by mid-August.
19. The final step is to print student schedules by mid-August and prepare for distribution.

OUTSIDE THE BOX THINKING

Guidelines for Creating the High School Master Schedule

It is very apparent in the "Planning the High School Master Schedule" checklist that there are a lot of steps and details to be followed to have a successful student-driven master schedule. As the high school principal, it is important to be a participant and active member in all the master schedule planning meetings. It is just as important that the principal keeps the master schedule team members on track when it comes to the information they need to work on and deadlines they need to meet.

Because the high school master schedule requires a lot of time and attention to detail, you will find the Guidelines for Creating the High School Master Schedule, Figure B.10, in appendix B extremely helpful. Along with your guidance department chair, you could organize the master schedule chart in the summer for the following year. The master schedule team should put all the dates in their calendar for the year, which gives everyone plenty of notice to work on their required parts of the schedule. It is important that the master schedule team honors the dates of the master schedule chart. Teachers always appreciate receiving their final teaching schedule for the upcoming school year before they leave for the summer.

Most of the master schedule building should take place on the all-day Friday and all-day Saturday time slots noted on the master schedule chart. This two-day meeting can prove to be productive as it is free of interruption with many consecutive hours to focus on the master schedule. Since Friday is a school day, your school resource officer or designated personnel could handle any issues so that you are not interrupted.

While building the master schedule if you experience conflict between when to offer certain classes, you could resolve it by having a discussion with your department chair. It is always helpful to have copies of the Teaching Assignment Sheets, Figure B.11, to know what subjects teachers are able to teach. This information provides not only the courses that teachers desire to teach but more importantly what they are certified to teach.

All members of your master schedule team should be professionally trained on whatever software platform you are using to build your master schedule.

ATHLETICS AND EXTRACURRICULAR ACTIVITIES

RATIONALE: An important aspect of the principal's duties is overseeing athletics and extracurricular activities. Research has proven that students who are involved in sports and/or extracurricular activities do better in school academically. While athletics are a vital part of higher-grade levels, extracurricular activities and community-sponsored clubs provide a wealth of value to students in the lower grade levels. Therefore, it is important that all sports and activities have quality leadership, are organized, and made available to your student body.

1. All sports, activities, and clubs require the board of education approval. Be sure to have a criminal background check done on all new hires (who are not current staff members) including coaches, assistant coaches, and advisors. This includes occasional volunteers who may support a club, band, or sports team.
2. At the middle and high school, meet with your athletic director and assistant principals to review the sports schedule for the school year. Assign which administrator(s) will be at each event. Be sure to follow guidelines on crowd control and how many administrators are required for highly attended events, for example, home football games.
3. There are many clubs in grades K-12, and some have paid advisors. Club advisor contracts are for one year at a time. At the end of each school year, teachers or staff can choose to renew their supplemental duties as a club advisor. *Be sure to post all club advisor openings and hire new advisors before the following school year.*
4. Create an extracurricular handbook online that includes a list of all clubs, requirements to join the club, advisors' names, contact information, and room location (if employed at your school). Often students may not join clubs especially as freshmen because they are either not aware of the club or unsure how to join or who to contact. Posting notices and making announcements can help notify students in K-8.
5. Assign one of your administrators (or an office person in the elementary or middle school) to keep track of all club activities along with fundraisers for each club to eliminate duplicating activities and fundraisers. Have each club advisor fill out a building permit form to streamline building facility use as well as custodial needs.
6. Once a month, meet with the student president of each club for an advisory. Have the students name this group, for example, the Principal's Leadership Group. These students will serve as your board of directors and can provide great insight into what is going on in the school. See *Outside the Box Thinking, Student Leadership Groups* that follows this checklist.

7. Know the budget for your clubs and activities. Be aware and support annual fundraising activities that have become a tradition in your school, for example, PTA annual sloppy joe dinner where the profit goes to student scholarship. Your athletic director will oversee the budget for all sports and an office person can coordinate budgeting for clubs and organizations.
8. Develop a system for input from athletes, coaches, participants, and club coordinators so that you can gain firsthand knowledge of any issues or celebratory items.
9. Set goals and targets for your athletic director that support your expectations for growth and improvement. Your athletic director should set goals for all head coaches. Participate in all head coach evaluations with your athletic director. This goes a long way with head coaches as it shows that you value and appreciate all they do for your student athletes and the school. Complete an annual evaluation of all clubs including club advisors' performances.
10. Athletics in middle and high school require a great deal of effort, planning, execution, and evaluation. It is important to meet with your athletic director every week to review the sporting events for the coming weekend to review time, location, and administrative coverage. Double check that all head coaches and club advisors have medical emergency release information on all students and that they take these forms to all events.
11. When necessary, your athletic director should be responsible for organizing the referee schedule for all home sporting events. Your head coaches should be responsible for ordering buses for all away events. It is the principal's role to know who is responsible for these assignments. Personnel responsible for these duties may vary by district.
12. You should have an athletic code of conduct, separate from your student code of conduct. Your athletic director is responsible for writing and updating the athletic code of conduct with your input. This document requires the board of education approval. Be sure that all student athletes as well as their parent/guardian sign and agree with the athletic code of conduct.

OUTSIDE THE BOX THINKING
STUDENT LEADERSHIP GROUPS

It is important as a principal to organize a student leadership group, at any grade level, to assist with decision making, student-led ideas, and to enhance school climate. As a principal, initiate a student leadership group that you could refer to as your "Board of Directors," and allow the students to name the group. This group could consist of presidents of your school's clubs and organizations who meet monthly to discuss various activities and to share ideas. During these monthly meetings, each student leader should update the group on their events. Afterward, you should discuss student concerns and ideas to make your school a better place.

With students in grades K-8, forming a principal's advisory group, or council, can be an effective way to keep your finger on the pulse of the student body. Volunteers, or students recommended by teachers, can serve on your council. It might be advisable to change students throughout the year so that you can become familiar with more representatives of the student body. It is also suggested that, as a principal, you choose the same time to meet with the group so that it is built into your schedule.

No matter how you configure your advisory group, establishing a purpose for the group is the most important thing. With councils, the main purpose should be to advise the principal of concerns or issues that might be bothering other students. One of the first things that the council can do in the elementary school is to create a Suggestion Box in a visible location. It can become the job of the advisors to read the suggestions and make a list of valid ones to bring to the council. These items could be discussed and determined together if they could be addressed as a group or by the principal.

The idea of the Suggestion Box can be initiated in middle school. The process for developing the Middle School Advisory Council would be different in that students could be invited to serve on the Council. Students who may not always have a voice may be chosen. This group can begin to take on a service component offering and implementing suggestions to improve the school climate, facilities, and operations. They can organize workdays to clean up the outside of the school and volunteer to assist at athletic events.

It is important to include an opportunity for evaluation at the end of each grading period. Everyone in grades K-8, who served on the council, could list things they liked, did not like and things that needed to be done in the future. It takes time to review these so that you could understand how the students are thinking. See *Committee Evaluation form, Figure B.12, in appendix B*.

The council can give you a great deal of contact with individual students that you normally would not have. It also can provide the students with another opportunity for leadership and involvement guided by an authority figure.

BEING A LEADER IN SPECIAL EDUCATION

RATIONALE: As a building principal, you will have many responsibilities that deal with personnel, facilities, finance, and students. But none may be as important as your leadership in special education. Sometimes counselors, school psychologists, department heads have primary responsibility for supervising the special education program, but it is essential that the principal is knowledgeable of the process and the people involved within the school. Take care to review this checklist of recommendations.

1. Learn the requirements of the Federal Regulations for Implementing Individuals with Disabilities Education Act (IDEA).
2. Know your Board of Education Policies regarding placements, discipline, accommodations, Individual Education Plans (IEPs), teacher qualifications, etc.
3. Create a team with teachers, aides, parents, counselors, and other personnel to best serve the special needs students in the school.
4. Be available and communicate with parents of students with special needs.
5. Respect confidentiality of meetings and conversations with parents, students, and teachers.
6. Review IEPs with teachers and counselors understanding accommodations for students and the principal's role in meeting those needs.
7. Develop a system for keeping anecdotal records of meetings and interactions with students and teachers. This is a valuable tool for reference.
8. Establish consistent and clear academic and behavioral expectations for your teachers and students. Practice being clear and fair with discipline and consequences.
9. Make visits to classrooms, recognize effective teaching practices and where students are learning. Be visible. Be a positive role model.
10. Meet with teachers to communicate about students. Head off problems with preventive tactics. Assist teachers with classroom management needs, instructional practices, behavioral expectations, and rule setting. See *Outside the Box Thinking, Special Education Ideas for Teachers* following this checklist.

OUTSIDE THE BOX THINKING
SPECIAL EDUCATION IDEAS FOR TEACHERS

The category of Special Education can encompass a wide range of student abilities and behaviors. Teachers need to remain flexible, committed, and willing to work with students, parents, and supporting personnel to best meet the needs of each student. As a principal, it is not only important to know what strategies and techniques can assist teachers in the special education setting, but it is essential to share and assist teachers to ensure classroom success. Strive for organization, structure, and routine with your students. Being prepared for lessons and activities helps to demonstrate consistency for your students in your classroom.

- Reflect on your teaching style. Face students when you talk, use eye contact and proximity to engage students. Limit direct instruction to 10-minute lessons followed by practice and application.
- Wait until the class is quiet and ready before giving directions. Explain clearly and slowly what expectations you have for the assignment. Follow verbal directions with written ones. Model what to do and show the class work samples from other students.
- Use multisensory instruction. Provide visual and verbal instructions to better meet the needs of the students. Include many opportunities for hands-on activities and projects.
- Post clear and concise rules in your classroom. Be consistent and fair in your consequences. Use positive reinforcement as much as possible.
- Be clear in your expectations of behavior, modeling appropriate behavior in and out of your classroom. Practice and reteach acceptable behaviors.
- Develop a system of private, personal cuing with students who need reminders. Positioning yourself near them or tapping the desk can help to refocus attention without disrupting the entire instructional process.
- Develop a system of consistent communication with the parents or guardians. Be sure this method is a two-way device so that parents can contact you as well. Share positive news as well as concerns. Having more frequent interactions can help to avoid problems that may occur.
- Respect confidentiality of written and verbal information regarding students and home situations. Share information with persons who need to know.
- Keep communications open between administrators, counselors, and classroom teachers. Use them as a sounding board or to help in problem-solving. Keep principals in the loop with troubled students or parents.

SUMMARY CHAPTER THREE
ORGANIZATION

The authors have placed the topic ORGANIZATION following others because organizational skills are a key to the successful operations of the school. Time management, planning, problem-solving, and team building can help to organize the entire school community. The principal is the leader and must strive to prepare for the school year and all the activities that constitute the calendar of events regardless of the grade levels or school configuration.

The organization is a relevant topic as it requires the principal to lead staff and students in collaborative efforts for the purpose of the development of a successful educational program. Key concepts in this chapter are:

- Getting ready for the school year is one of the most important organizational tasks for the principal. It involves communication with all the

stakeholders and organizing all aspects of the school program to better serve the students.
- Opening of school should include meetings, not just with teachers, but with support staff to share expectations, practices, schedules, and procedures for the year.
- Organizing a system of student discipline begins with each teacher creating a written discipline plan that includes rules, procedures, consequences, and positive reinforcement.
- In all schools, much time is devoted to developing and implementing a master schedule. The role of the principal may vary between grade levels and schools, but an important factor is to have a representative team of staff to assist with the process.
- Athletics and extracurricular activities require organization on the part of the principal. Meetings with advisors, administrators, or parent volunteers are important to successfully plan calendars, adequate supervision, and facilities.
- The principal should develop and meet with a council of students involved in activities to develop a code of conduct and a platform for future reciprocal interactions.
- As the instructional leader of the school, the principal must be knowledgeable of the laws, policies, and regulations governing special education. Much organization is needed to monitor students, records, expectations, and teaching practices for special needs students.

INSIDE-THE-SCHOOL SUCCESS
READER'S THOUGHTS ON THE TOPIC

Reflection is an important part of being a leader. Following your reading, take time to assess the information and consider its meaning and usefulness to you as a principal. Before moving on to the next topic, take time to reflect on the topics you just completed. After reviewing the lists and the supportive materials, choose at least two items and explain how you would use this information in your leadership role to ensure school success and create an Award-Winning School.

_____
_____
_____
_____
_____

Review the *Outside the Box Thinking* included after the checklist pages and the appendix items. Think about how you might use a technique now or in the future in your leadership role. Place your thoughts below on how you may implement this technique or how you might alter the technique to suit your role as a leader.

_____
_____
_____
_____
_____

Be sure to save your thoughts on this topic for future reference. Try to share something new with a colleague or staff member.

NOTES

1. Schoenlein, "Intervention Assistance Teams in Ohio," *American Secondary Education*, Vol. 20, No 2 (1991):27–30.

2. DuFour, Richard and Rebecca and Robert Eaker, "Whatever it Takes," Solutions Tree, 2004. go.SolutionsTree.com/PLC books.

3. DuFour and Eaker. "Whatever It Takes."

4. Schoenlein, "Intervention Assistance Teams in Ohio."

5. Brown-Chidsey, Rachel and Mark W. Steege, "Response to Intervention," 2004. http://www.rtinetwork.org/learn/what/whatisrti.

Chapter 4

Operations

Developing the Processes that Operate Your School for Inside-the-School Success

This is a relevant topic because all the skills included in the checklists for ONESELF, OTHERS, and ORGANIZATION are combined to enable the principal to successfully deal with the day-to-day operations of the school. School OPERATIONS deal with the Safety and Security of the facility and the persons within. A major responsibility for the operations of the school is Personnel Management. This involves recruitment, hiring, mentoring, and evaluating teachers and support staff.

School Operations are enhanced through the principal's knowledge of budgeting and finance and crisis management. Implementation and supervision of the use of technology is an expanding role for the principal. All these areas should include faculty and staff in the understanding of policies, procedures, and execution of the operations.

While the opening of school was covered under ORGANIZATION, closing of school is included in operations. The principal must rely on skills to involve all members of the staff and student body to prepare for the close of the current school year while planning to open the next school year. This is an important topic because it requires the principal to rely on learned skills to guide all stakeholders.

ENSURING THE SECURITY AND SAFETY OF YOUR SCHOOL

RATIONAL: The principal must ensure that the building and its inhabitants are safe and secure to guarantee an enhanced learning environment. Many factors can be safety hazards such as building internal maintenance issues, outside storms, flooding, power outages, accidents, student bullying, harassment, intruders, bomb threats, etc. To prepare for safety and security issues the principal must be educated and work as part of a team. Read through this list and reflect on the suggestions made by other administrators.

1. Locate and review the safety plan for your school and your district. Post-school rules and consequences throughout the school. Share with students and parents.
2. Become familiar with state law and district policies regarding security and safety in the schools.
3. Identify the leaders in the safety process and meet with them (these may be within your school or in the community). Communicate roles in the process to all personnel in the school.
4. Clarify your role as part of the safety team. What responsibilities do you have in day-to-day operations? What responsibilities do you have in emergency situations?
5. Identify safety issues within your school. Walk the building with support personnel and list areas of concern; for example, crowded hallways, poor kitchen facilities, unlocked exits, etc.
6. Enroll in in-service or training opportunities regarding safety and security.
7. Schedule regular meetings with your safety team to review policies and safety concerns. As a team, plan and execute effective drills for tornado, fire, active shooter, and evacuation.
8. Identify, establish, and enforce new rules and policies that prohibit unacceptable behaviors and the consequences of severe behaviors such as assault, tobacco and alcohol use, bullying, social media abuse, and other criminal acts.
9. Provide faculty and students in service on the new rules and policies and the consequences for inappropriate behavior.
10. Work as an entire school to make safety a priority. Have counselors and teachers share information about troubled students who may be bullied, harassed, or display warning signs of aggressive behavior or hostilities.

CRISIS MANAGEMENT

RATIONALE: Along with the Safety and Security of your school facilities and community, the principal must be prepared to handle a crisis. What causes a crisis? A crisis can be a situation in or out of the school that is unexpected, critical, and has emotional significance to all or part of the school community. There can be internal causes such as threats, shootings, intruders, student illness, and outside causes such as injury, death, disease, natural disasters, and pandemics. Dealing with incidences can be difficult. Systematic planning can help administrative teams to adequately prepare for a variety of crises.

1. While a crisis occurs unexpectedly, planning can be done in advance to anticipate problems that may occur leading to a crisis. Build a rapport with parents and students so that they have confidence and trust in your decision-making.
2. No matter what the cause of your crisis, rely on your safety team to serve in a crisis intervention role for support and advice. Consult your school safety plan.
3. For shared decision making, consult experts from within (like counselors, psychologists, other administrators) and from without (police, fire, health, and medical personnel, etc.)
4. Crises can develop from within. Student groups or individuals can be the origin of disruptive behavior leading to an internal crisis. Use your Intervention Assistance Team which is explained in chapter 3 to analyze student behavior within the school.
5. Offer staff members training in recognizing troubled children. Work to locate children with problems and provide interventions. Rely on the expertise of trained professionals to assist.
6. Your school facility and surrounding grounds can also be a cause of a crisis. Assess your school facilities' preparedness for a crisis, eliminating hazards and securing outside entrances, and implementing security measures.
7. Work to secure your school neighborhood for safety considerations, dangerous persons, or situations that may escalate to bigger issues. Work with police and school safety personnel to alter situations in advance.
8. Often a crisis requires instant decision making and strong leadership skills. Rely on your poise, and problem-solving, decision-making skills presented in chapter 1.
9. If the crisis is one that is evolving, like the pandemic or a chemical spill or severe weather experience, the leader must reach out to district personnel, state officials, medical officials, and personnel that are experts in their fields.
10. Time limits may not be a consideration in making educated decisions when entire districts and regions are involved in the crisis. Carefully considering advice from professionals can aid in the problem-solving necessary to solve more global crises. This would be a time to share information and decision-making with district personnel, city and county safety officials, health experts, and the community in general. No matter what the situation is, it is important to centralize your communication; for example, your superintendent would host a media conference.

… Chapter 4

PERSONNEL MANAGEMENT
HIRING, MENTORING, AND EVALUATING
YOUR TEACHING STAFF

RATIONALE: An essential part of the principal's duties is the hiring, mentoring, and evaluating of the teaching staff. The year-long process allows the principal to select and assist staff in improving teaching and learning. Check with your superintendent regarding the process for hiring and recruiting. While hiring may involve other personnel within the district, the responsibility of mentoring and evaluating falls to the building level administrator(s). It is critical to follow the required evaluation protocol including timelines and procedures, to effectively implement the process.

1. When you can hire new teachers, seek out candidates that have a similar educational philosophy to you and your district. See *Reference Check Form, Figure C.1 in appendix C*.
2. When hiring new teachers, form an interview committee that includes principal, assistant principal(s), and department chair or teachers in the content which you are hiring. For second-round interviews, it is important to have each candidate do a thirty-minute lesson for the committee. See *Interview Worksheet, Figure C.2 in appendix C* for sample interview questions.
3. It would be ideal to have all hiring completed by early spring as that will ensure better candidates. Interviews should take place after school or on Saturdays so that the operations of school can take place during the school day. But be prepared to hire throughout the summer and even up until school begins.
4. New teachers will be involved in district-wide orientations and mentoring programs. The principal is responsible for building-level orientations and mentoring. A major portion of this should focus on the evaluation process so that new hires will have a complete understanding and rely on the principal(s) for assistance in the classroom.
5. For teacher evaluation, prior to the beginning of the school year, secure a copy of the teachers' contract and become familiar with the guidelines and the principal's responsibilities.
6. Meet with other principals (if available in your school) and divide your teaching staff amongst your administrative team. Notify your teachers who their evaluator is in writing at the Opening teachers' meeting.
7. Provide a faculty inservice session on the importance of the evaluation process to enable teachers to be partners with you in making instructional improvements. Share your procedures, priorities, and instructional strategies and accept input from teachers so that evaluation is a growth

opportunity and not a surprise. It is important to be aware of all the hard work your teachers do outside the classroom. See *Professional Development Record and Highlights, Figure C.3 in appendix C* as a guide.
8. Create a chart that lists all teachers and each administrator completing the evaluation including timelines of observations, walkthroughs, and year-end evaluation. See *The Teacher Evaluation Chart, Figure C.4 in appendix C*.
9. When possible, assign your administrative team to evaluate teachers in the same content they taught as a teacher. If you are the only administrator, you will need to serve as an evaluator and a mentor to your staff. See *Outside the Box Thinking, The Principal as a Mentor* following this checklist.
10. Follow district policy as to the annual recommendation of teachers who qualify for contract renewal or continuing contract (this depends on your district). One of the reasons evaluation timelines are so important is that a teacher could be given a contract renewal because an administrator did not follow the evaluation timelines and procedures.
11. Know the procedures (according to your teacher contract) that need to be followed for teachers who may need to be put on an improvement plan. Meet with your superintendent or supervisors to be sure you understand the required procedures for the improvement plan. Pay attention to all due dates even in an "off-year," evaluation.
12. Consult chapter 2 on Becoming the Instructional Leader for suggestions to assist classroom teachers.

OUTSIDE THE BOX THINKING
THE PRINCIPAL AS A MENTOR

The principal is the instructional leader of the school community and serves an important role in being a mentor to new teachers. This role also extends to teachers changing subject areas, buildings or grade levels, or teachers who may be having trouble with instruction. While most states require an assigned mentor from the teaching ranks, this does not preclude the principal from helping all teachers within the school.

The role of the Principal as a Mentor should support the goal of high-quality learning and instruction resulting in the success of every student in the school. Some of the characteristics of a principal as an effective mentor:

- Be secure and confident in his/her instructional abilities and able to model or share these abilities with others.
- Have an insight into the day-to-day operations of the school while grasping the total school program.

- Interact, share, listen, and problem solve with teachers with the goal of improving instruction and student learning.
- Exhibit self-confidence as an instructor and model that trait for new and experienced teachers.
- Study the teaching process and search for resources to assist teachers.
- Develop reflective practices and model these through problem-solving models so that teachers may become reflective and self-directed through discussion and questioning of instruction.
- Find ways to help teachers through:
  - Direct assistance by problem-solving with the teacher.
  - Sharing demonstrations of effective teaching practices through observation or video.
  - Participating in peer reflection through sharing with other teachers about the class or teaching practices.
  - Indirect or informal contact through walk-through observations.
  - Informal sharing at lunch or conference time.
  - Role modeling by watching others teach parts of a lesson that might be difficult for the teacher.
  - Recording parts of the lesson and analyzing and discussing improvements.

The principal should work closely with teacher mentors in your building. Teachers should be given a chance to shine in front of their peers. The principal should attend formal and informal meetings and in-service training with the teachers to gain insight into the interaction between teachers and mentors. Make instructional improvements a goal for your school and focus in-service training on ways that the entire staff can benefit from formal and informal mentoring.

SCHOOL BUDGETING AND FINANCE

RATIONALE: Each school district/building may have different procedures for principals to follow to utilize the school budgeting process. Some districts will have totally centralized budgeting that allows for little discretion on the part of the building administrator. Other districts may have a system of decentralization that provides a large building budget, leaving the principal with accounting for most of the purchases and hires. Also, there is a great difference between grade level configurations for budgeting. The high school and middle school may have athletic and special operating funds to support extracurricular activities and programs that may not be found in the elementary school. *As a principal, it is your responsibility to learn about the process of financing for the district and your building.* Follow the guidelines below to help you to be an effective accountant for your school.

1. The information on finance that you will need begins in the interview process. Be prepared to ask questions about the district's financial security and process. What sources provide revenue for the schools? Does the district have levies that need to be renewed by voters? This information will have an impact on your building's appropriations.
2. Learn who is responsible for the accounting in your individual school. Some districts have administrative assistants, athletic secretaries, or human resources personnel who deal with parts of the budgeting process. See *Outside the Box Thinking, Building Level Budgeting* following this checklist.
3. Meet with the district treasurer or chief financial officer to learn how funds are appropriated to your building. (Some schools will be granted a per-pupil amount at the beginning of the school year). Ask questions about the procedures that are required for budgeting even if you are not the primary person dealing with the budget. It is important that you implement correct procedures that follow district policies.
4. Take time to learn how your district personnel view and account for discretionary spending, such as the principal's account. Some districts promote fundraising, and some do not. It is up to you to find out how this is done district wide and how you can or cannot implement it in your school.
5. Be knowledgeable about other departments in your district that oversee funds for the programs and personnel in your school. Federal funds provided for special education and vocational education programs may not be under your accounting, but it is important that you understand who oversees these accounts. At the higher-grade levels, there may be more accounts that are under your supervision but fall under another person's accounting.
6. Determine what other financial resources are provided for your school. Are there grants governing programs or personnel? If there are, you must be familiar with the persons involved and in charge of the funding and the renewal of the grant.
7. It is important that you know other organizations that may provide support for your building. In some districts, parent–teacher organizations and community or corporate groups may provide direct financial support to your school. The principal must have an awareness of all groups and how the funding is given to the school. Are items purchased for the school? Are funds used to support a program and donated to the treasurer's office? Learn how these funds are acquired, recognized, and distributed. This is essential information for the building administrator.

8. Be aware of all accounts that fall under your building supervision. Many schools will have activity accounts for student clubs and organizations. These require the principal's knowledge especially if fundraising is involved.
9. Determine the system for use of discretionary funds such as petty cash or the principal's fund. This will probably be an account directly under your supervision. Understand who has access to the spending, how it is done (credit card, and reimbursement), and if and where funds are stored in the school.
10. In recent years, some teachers and personnel have initiated Go Fund Me pages or other technology programs to raise funds for their classrooms. As a principal, examine this practice and determine the board of education or governing board's policies on these types of fundraisers. What is the principal's role in the process and oversight of funds?
11. As with other administrative duties, plan a system for organizing and monitoring the spending for your school. Examine current practices, interview persons involved in your building spending, and accept and implement recommendations for changes in practices if needed.
12. Build time into your schedule to work with building-level persons involved in ordering, spending, processing, and dealing with school district funds. Budgeting is a year-long process that requires constant oversight and planning. *Regardless of who oversees the budgeting and funds in your school, you, the principal, are responsible for the operation to work effectively.*

OUTSIDE THE BOX THINKING

Building Level Budgeting

A sound principle for dealing with finance is to be sure that you are aware of spending within your school. The process of budgeting may vary from school to school or district to district. In some situations, you may need to relinquish control of parts of your budget to department heads, athletic directors, and persons in quasi-administrative positions. The most important thing is to know and understand the accepted practices in your school district. Once you are aware of these, you can establish an organized system of accounting for your school.

An emphasis for school budgeting would be that the principal, regardless of the grade level, "keeps the reigns" on spending and is somewhat frugal regarding the total budget. Also, one would be advised to be as fair and equitable when giving department chairs or unified arts a budget line. They all talk so it is important to have a rule of thumb that you follow (ex: each unified arts teacher in my building gets X amount of dollars per pupil). Some departments in your school, such as special education, may have a district-wide budget.

Another consideration may be the purchase of items such as desks, tables, whiteboards, computers, and other items that would be considered non-consumables. These may come from a separate budget for the entire district. Once you have determined which items fall in your school budget you can consider staff requests and prioritize the total needs of your school to allocate your funds.

To assess spending and predict your budget for the entire year, a secretary or administrative assistant could serve as a finance resource person. This person could supervise the day-to-day allocations, purchasing, and oversight of all things related to money. However, the principal may request that all spending goes through him/her first, especially teacher requests for items. Meeting with the building finance resource person regularly could help to determine what levels of spending have been completed and what resources are left in the budget as the school year progresses.

Some principals may wish to save big purchases for near the end of the year; however, your district treasurer may prefer that budget money be used and spent sooner. This might constitute a change to your practices. An important piece of advice would be if you get a new treasurer, meet with him/her to learn if the budgeting process would remain the same or change. Some districts may change the entire budgeting process based on the philosophy of new central office personnel. This makes it essential for the principal to remain current in budgeting practices that pertain to the building level.

IMPLEMENTATION, EDUCATION, AND EVALUATION OF SCHOOL TECHNOLOGY

RATIONALE: As a school leader, you should expect your teachers and students to be progressive with technology. You need to do the same and lead by example. Not only do you have the role in oversight of the use of technology, but you also have the challenge of integrating resources into your own day to facilitate your duties and responsibilities. The purpose of this topic is not to highlight types of technology software but rather to stress the principal's role in implementing and evaluating the use of technology.

1. All administrators, teachers, staff, and students should sign your board of education approved acceptable use policy for technology. It is important to have all new students who enroll after the beginning of the school year sign the form as well.
2. All administrators, teachers, staff, and students should be educated on the appropriate use of technology and the consequences should technology not be used

appropriately. Dedicate a staff in-service day to the use/misuse of technology by staff and students.
3. Hire a speaker on technology to present to your student body. The speaker should be current with technology including all forms of social media. The presentation would include communicating the negative impact it has on individual students and schools like cyberbullying. This same speaker could do a similar presentation for the parents. See *Outside of the Box Thinking, Training for Technology* following this checklist.
4. Have your School Resource Officer communicate to your school community the legal ramifications of inappropriate use of technology. Be sure to include an article regarding technology from your School Resource Officer in your principal's newsletter. Continue to send reminders to students and parents throughout the school year.
5. As a principal, try to utilize all forms of technology to communicate to your school community. Including but not limited to: E-mail, Twitter, Facebook, Webpage, Google Meet, Google Docs, and Zoom.
6. If possible, assign interested teachers to oversee Facebook, and your school's web page, as a supplemental duty.
7. Stay current with technology software that is available to manage your school more efficiently. Attendance and grading software, student data for I-phone, emergency contact information, and teacher evaluation software can assist you in your day-to-day operations.
8. Support staff development training for content-specific software that improves teaching and learning. To save costs, send one or two teachers to a workshop and they, in turn, can train the rest of their department.
9. Electronic school security software should be a focus for the entire school district. Be sure to share your thoughts and concerns on this subject with the safety officers, superintendent, and anyone who has the authority to purchase the best software possible that you can within your budget.
10. It is essential that schools have a hotline and a method of communicating to the parents and community for emergencies. A tip line should be available for the district or school so that important information can be shared anonymously with school or safety personnel.

OUTSIDE THE BOX THINKING
TRAINING FOR TECHNOLOGY

Because technology is constantly evolving especially with social media it is important as a school leader to have annual (or at least every two years) school assemblies with expert speakers on this topic. The impact of social media, both positively and negatively, on young people cannot be underestimated. Various forms of technology especially social media can drastically impact your overall school climate, for example, issues of cyberbullying. Therefore, as a school leader, it is important to take the stance of being proactive and provide as much information as possible on the appropriate use of technology.

When it comes to technology today, parents can become confused because of the ongoing changes to education. A technology speaker could present to your parent group the history of the internet and social networking. The speaker could provide information and tactics parents can use to keep their kids safe in the online world. Topics include social networking, E-scams, Cyber Bullying, Identify Theft, and Sexting. Furthermore, the speaker could discuss the effect that social networking sites can have on a student's ability to get a job or get into college as well as how students can protect their image and prevent people from getting the wrong idea from content found on their personal online profiles.

In addition, principals need to look internally to develop experts to help all stakeholders to understand the importance of proper technology usage. If you are in an elementary school, it might become necessary to have a teacher or staff member receive special training in the legal responsibilities of technology use and schools. This person can serve as a resource to other teachers and parents by providing face-to-face meetings and printed articles online or in the school newsletter.

Your School Resource Officer or school technology personnel are an excellent resource for communicating the legal ramifications of the inappropriate use of technology. School Resource Officers could present to your students and parents the negative impact of social networking in a variety of ways such as individual classroom presentations, individual student meetings, class assemblies, PTA meetings, school-wide parent groups, and individual parent meetings.

Your School Resource Officer or school technology personnel could have a column in your school newsletter where they highlight topics such as cyberbullying, social networking, and "sexting." By utilizing these experts as an educational resource your students will not see them as someone who is "out to get them," but rather someone who is there to help them maneuver their way through school in a healthy way.

During parent-teacher conferences, open houses, or other school-wide events, your School Resource Officer or technology expert can be in attendance to answer social networking questions along with a table available of helpful literature. In addition, you could have a school webpage that highlights hot topics such as the negative impact of social networking.

END OF THE YEAR PREPARATIONS

RATIONALE: The end of the school year is a busy time in all buildings with ceremonies, celebrations, and field trips impacting the school day. This also is a time for the administrator to reflect on the past year and look forward to the new school year to follow. The most essential strategy for preparing is to be organized and to work to organize your staff and students. The following list can help you have a smooth closing of the school year:

1. At the end of each school year work with office personnel to prepare an online master calendar of important dates for the following school year:
   - field trips;
   - awards assemblies and graduation;
   - testing;
   - early release dates; and
   - failure letters, closing of grades, and report cards.

   Include in your calendar, important due dates for teachers (testing, grades closing, exam and early release dates, failure letter mailings, etc.)

2. Share this calendar with staff, parents, and students and provide a narrative to emphasize important final dates for all.
3. Prior to grades closing, counselors and office staff should assist teachers in preparations for final testing and grades. Teachers should notify all parents of student failures and turn in a failure list by grade level to guidance counselors or office staff in charge. Failure forms will be used to answer parent calls, adjust future schedules due to failures, arrange parent conferences or enroll students in summer school.
4. As a principal, work with counselors and office staff to prepare teachers for the last workday of school. It is important that on your teacher's last day of work that they complete required forms and turn in materials so that a smooth transition can take place at the beginning of the following school year. See *End of the Year Check-out list, Figure C.5, in appendix C*.
5. Prior to the last day of school, teachers should collect and check textbooks and store them in designated locations. Teachers should determine the conditions of the books and fill out the textbook inventory sheet which includes book rebinds, lost/damaged, and replacement price. Textbook inventory sheets should be turned into the designated administrator or office personnel so that books can be taken care of over the summer.
6. When final exams are a part of the year-end calendar, teachers should turn in all corrected final exams to the designated administrator or office personnel. All corrected final exams should be labeled with the teacher's name, grade level, subject, period, along with a grading scale. This information is helpful to have over the summer in case parents have a discrepancy with a final exam grade. Students needing to make up exams should be noted on a separate list and kept in a folder with the same information labeled.

7. Teachers should turn in all keys along with their identification badge which is checked by your head custodian. Keys should be made available for teachers with extended time or coaching responsibilities. It would be important to create a key inventory and identification badge form which includes: Teacher's name, identification badge, room keys, key number, and room number.
8. Teachers are responsible for their own classrooms at the closing of the school year. All custodial work orders and summer maintenance request forms should be submitted to the office. The room should be organized, and materials stored to prepare for summer cleaning.
9. Teachers should turn in their classroom management plan to their designated administrator or office personnel. This ensures that grading policies, classroom expectations, and parent communication have been explained for the incoming class. Classroom management plans should be approved by your administrative team before they have been copied and readied for distribution to students the following school year. See *Classroom Management Plan Assessment form, in appendix B.*
10. All Individual Education Plans (IEP's) should be turned into the designated administrator or office staff for filing.
11. If available, teachers can be provided with their up-to-date teaching schedule for the following year. The office should also obtain teachers' summer contact information in case it is needed.
12. In preparing for the close of school, the principal should consider providing staff with an evaluation form or an opportunity to assess the school year and his/her performance as a building principal. This is an excellent opportunity for you to reflect with your office staff and counselors and review comments by the teaching staff. See *Outside the Box Thinking, Principal's Year-End Collaborative Assessment Form* following this checklist.

REFLECTIONS AT THE END OF THE YEAR

As the school year draws to a close in all schools, the principal is provided an opportunity to reflect on the events of the finished year. In addition, this reflective time should have another purpose. Along with assessing the closing year, one should be looking forward to the next school year as well.

How can the principal gain, assess and implement thoughts, criticisms, and suggestions from the stakeholders in the school building?

One suggestion is to begin with a review of the content that was presented in chapter 1, Oneself, at the beginning of this book. The focus in that chapter was to assist the principal in developing self-reflection, self-assessment, and self-confidence to better lead the staff and students at the school.

In chapter 1, the reflective practices that were presented included:

- focusing on solving problems,
- establishing personal and professional goals,
- developing a personal mission statement, and
- implementing self-evaluation techniques.

A thorough review of one's personal and professional goals and personal mission statement can assist the leader in self-reflection. This could be an essential step in effective self-analysis by the principal. Measuring one's own professional growth and performance can help to prepare the psyche for opening the door to the opinions and thoughts of others. This is not an easy process. This review should be planned with time allotted to reflect and revisit events and issues from the current year as the leader looks toward the future.

After self-reflection, the principal should decide from whom input is needed. Before the staff and students leave for the summer, it is a chance to gain some insight from others with whom you have worked.

Gaining input can be done through small group meetings from student and faculty advisory groups that are already in place. The group can utilize guided questions included in *Outside The Box Thinking, Principal's Year-End Collaborative Assessment*. This would be an opportunity for the members to give oral feedback or written responses to be reviewed later.

In addition, the Year-End Collaborative Assessment can be given to all staff to seek input on past school operations. This process would provide written feedback to the principal. It can also help to develop reflective practices in the teachers and staff as they review the events and issues of the past school year.

A suggestion could be that the principal review these forms with the administrative team, administrative assistant, lead teachers, or guidance personnel that form the office support network. Having a brainstorming session can help the leader to decipher the responses and create a more analytical approach to gaining and measuring input from many sources.

The review of input should be systematic using charts, post its, eraser boards, etc. with a group. While input is important, the assessment of that input is essential to the overall success of evaluation.

As the leader, the principal should decide:

- who should be involved in analysis,
- how the information will be used,
- how problems will be identified and resolved,
- how the information will be deciphered to the stakeholders, and
- how goals will be set for the future.

Including varied personnel in the evaluation process can be as important as the results. Reflection is important at the end of the year to help the building level principal to improve the operations of the school and to chart a path to success for the future.

OUTSIDE THE BOX THINKING PRINCIPAL'S YEAR-END COLLABORATIVE ASSESSMENT

To assist in performance reflections, please take the time to provide valuable written feedback to your principal.

The purpose of this document is for the principal to gain insight into the perceptions of staff to aid in making improvements to the overall school operations. This will enable goals to be set for the next school year based on your feedback. This is an optional survey and will remain anonymous. Thank you for taking the time to participate.

1. What strengths have you observed in your principal?

2. In what areas would you see that the principal may need improvement?

3. In the past school year, what did you like best about your school?

4. What would you like to see changed about your school or in the principal's role in your school?

Please take time to add additional comments below regarding the survey, then return it to the office. Many thanks!

SUMMARY CHAPTER FOUR
OPERATIONS

Developing the Processes that Operate Your School for Inside-the-School Success

Chapter Four presented topics that support the completion of the day-to-day operations of the school. Administrative tasks that were covered rely on the skills previously learned in the first three chapters. A key role for the leader is to involve all members of the school community in working together to achieve success.

An area of operations includes safety and security of the school facilities, personnel, and students within. This has become an even more important focus for principals of schools in recent years. Not only is safety and security a prime responsibility for the management of personnel but the entire process of recruiting, hiring, mentoring, and evaluating staff falls to the building leader.

Budgeting and finance, classroom management and student discipline, and technology and instruction are included under school operations. These daily challenges require leaders to rely on a variety of skills to ensure that all operations of the school support teaching and learning.

Key concepts from chapter 4 include:

- Leaders should be sure to stay current on safety laws and regulations and consult regularly with district and community personnel on these issues.
- Interviewing, hiring, and mentoring teachers are an essential part of personnel management. The most important part of the role of instructional leader is always mentoring all staff.
- Technology is more important today than ever before in schools. Leaders should be familiar with district policies and procedures regarding student and staff usage in school and in the home as it relates to school interactions.
- Organization of staff and students is important to end-of-the-year readiness. The closing of the school is a process that begins early. Preparations include special events and procedures necessary to transition out of the current year and into the next school year.
- As a principal, it is your responsibility to learn about the process of financing for the district and your building. Learn who is responsible for the accounting in your individual school. Be knowledgeable about other departments in your district that oversee funds for the programs and personnel in your school.
- An essential element is to provide written evaluation forms for staff to assess yearly performance. Input is necessary on school events, procedures, and administrative performances throughout the year.

- Reflection at the close of school can be an important tool for planning for the future. The purpose of an evaluation document is for the principal to gain insight into the perceptions of staff. This can aid in making improvements to the overall school operations and to develop goals for the next school year.

INSIDE-THE-SCHOOL SUCCESS READER'S THOUGHTS ON THE CHECKLIST

Reflection is an important part of being a leader. Following your reading, take time to assess the information and consider its meaning and usefulness to you as a principal. Before moving on to the next topic, take time to reflect on the topics you just completed. After reviewing the lists and the supportive materials, choose at least two items and explain how you would use them in your leadership role to ensure school success and Create an Award-Winning School.

_____
_____
_____
_____

Review the *Outside the Box Thinking* included after the checklists and items in appendix C to determine how you might use a technique now or in the future in your leadership role. Place your thoughts below on how you may implement this technique or how you might alter the technique to suit your role as a leader.

_____
_____
_____
_____

Be sure to save your thoughts on this topic for future reference. Try to share something new with a colleague or staff member.

Chapter 5

Outreach

Developing Outside Networks and Gaining Effective Practices for Inside-the-School Success

An important part of this book is the inclusion of techniques and ideas from the current field of school administration. This section, entitled OUTREACH, is included to illustrate to principals the need for networking and the benefits of connecting to other administrators.

Why is informal networking important to the principal? The need is great for the building leader to develop a circle of peers and mentors inside and outside of the school. They can provide support as they understand the scope of the position. Everyone the principal meets professionally can be of help.

Who should be in this educational network? The leader should start with people he/she already knows, for example, alumni groups, college professors, and fellow graduate students who may also be in administrative positions. An important segment should be the other school district administrators who know the area and can provide valuable information and history to new personnel.

Looking to the community around the school may provide some connections that can assist the leader in predicting issues and problems before they occur. Community leaders and parents can be a vital part of a network also. The leader must be confident and willing to make the connections that can benefit him/her and the school as well.

As the principal develops the outreach component, self-reflection can assist in determining attributes he/she can provide for other persons in the network. Offering to speak about school programs at community meetings and college classes can be a valuable experience and help to pave a two-way street for the school. An additional avenue is provided by the state, regional, or national administrative organizations who have conferences, workshops, websites, and publications to enhance personal and professional knowledge.

The authors deemed it essential to incorporate suggestions and practices from principals, assistant principals, and district administrators to enhance the checklists and reflections presented in the book. Each idea that is presented in this chapter is from a former or practicing principal in grades K-12. The administrators who provided the input for this chapter are part of the extended network of the authors. The ideas were compiled from interactions through years of school leadership and college-level teaching. Their thoughts were selected by the authors as sound suggestions to promote the development of an Award-Winning School. Under the appropriate chapter title, ideas were placed to support the topics ONESELF, OTHERS, ORGANIZATION, and OPERATIONS. Following each idea is the principal's name with full recognition following in the bibliography.

It is hopeful that by sharing methods currently used in the field of school administration, the authors will exemplify the materials. It is important to note that a successful experience in the field of administration, especially for beginning principals, can be ensured through the development of a strong network.

IDEAS FROM THE FIELD OF EDUCATIONAL ADMINISTRATION OUTSIDE THE BOX THINKING CHAPTER ONE—ONESELF

The first chapter of this book includes concepts to promote personal strengths and wellbeing. This topic and the following suggestions from current and former principals in the field reinforce the need for self-assessment, organization, and reflection.

- GOAL SETTING—This document is used to keep track of administrative goals for the principal evaluation with the superintendent at the end of the school year. The document contains your goal statement that is aligned to the correlating principal standard, these are shared at the beginning of the year with your superintendent or evaluator. The Measures/Evidence (Products) section of the document is a running document for the year. I input different documents, PDF's, and articles that support work towards accomplishing my goals for the school year. At the end of the year, I share this document with my superintendent/evaluator and reflect on if goals were met. *See Administrative Goals, Figure D.1 in appendix D.*[1] (T.J. Ebert, Principal)
- GOAL SETTING—I learned so much in the six years I was principal. Upon reflection, I feel that a big takeaway for me professionally was goal setting. The first being a school-wide common goal, beliefs that we as a staff felt

important. The document on our school principles is a capture of the beliefs we as a staff developed, revised, and held sacred continuously. *See Basic Principles of Elementary Life, Figure D.2, in appendix D.*[2] (A Mcglenn, Principal)

- GOAL SETTING—Being a principal means wearing many different hats each day. Some days you will find yourself being a counselor, a disciplinarian, the maintenance director, safety officer, public relations person; the list could go on and on. Being able to handle the stress of it all is what can help make principals successful. One way I deal with stress is to stay organized. Making lists of things that need to be done each day and working through that list. Do what you can each day and then start again tomorrow. It is important to know that you do not have to do it all each day, just do your best. Prioritizing tasks has really helped with that.[3] (H. Mueller, Principal)
- PERSONAL BEHAVIOR—I would build a systematic communication practice with the superintendent or your direct supervisor. This is important early on in principalship to ensure that you are leading within the expectations of the district and have support from your superintendent during difficult decisions.[4] (B. Bontempo, Superintendent)
- PERSONAL BEHAVIOR—I learned many years ago, that taking on the role of principal can be a joyful personal and professional growth experience as you expand your world of caring for students, and their families as well as the larger community in which you are leading. It is also a privilege and a joy to lead teachers into a trusting community focused on professional learning. Today, I educate, encourage, and accelerate high-quality aspirational leaders to take on those roles; it remains to be the most joyful and satisfying personal and professional experience to see them blossom into leaders prepared to meet the challenges and expectations of our current global context.[5] (D. Morin, Director)
- PROBLEM SOLVING—Problem-solving is a strength that each administrator needs to embrace. The daily challenges of a school or school district are to deal with conflicts as they arise in a timely manner. Trying to identify the problem and listening to the concerns of the individual is the first step in the process. Be sure to have an open mind to what the issue is and where this is going. Try not to act swiftly by delivering the short or quick answer that you have in mind. The key is to be patient and sympathetic to the person making the problem known by being an engaged listener and taking notes of the conversation. Let the person know that this is something that will take a little time in looking into and is not something that will be put off for another day. Unless this is an emergency that affects the life and safety of others which constitutes mandatory reporting or police involvement immediately, look to begin the action steps you feel are important to problem-solving.

Interviewing of others will need to take place where the administrator needs to spend time prior to the meeting identifying questions that will help in first making sure that the problem is in fact accurate. When this has been established, it will allow the administrator to begin providing constructive feedback and solutions to the individual or individuals who made the problem known. Follow up can be in person or in a written form identifying the problem and how the solution came to be instituted. If there is a follow-up needed, then this can be rescheduled for another time to address any other or future concerns as well as how the solution is in fact going.[6] (R. Coxon, Assistant Principal)

- PROBLEM SOLVING—Our home is not a perfect place. We have issues every day. But what household doesn't? The best thing we have going for us is that we have so many creative minds to help us overcome and support one another when we face obstacles. When the custodian said, "I hate Thursdays; they are the messy lunch days (tacos, nachos, spaghetti . . .)," we spent time teaching how to eat a messy lunch and how to clean up our places before lining up. Every Thursday is now the "Messy Lunch Challenge" to see which grade level can leave the cafeteria the cleanest! When we see a problem, we teach, reteach, set goals, and celebrate.[7] (L. Stark, Principal)
- STRESS—Take time to self-evaluate, analyze interruptions and events that may be causing your stress. Ask reflective questions of yourself. *What am I spending most of my time on? When am I most stressed? Who may be causing my stress?* Think about remedies for the issues you have discovered. You may be able to self-evaluate to eliminate some of the stress.[8] (J. Filomena, Principal)
- STRESS—I am proud to say that I wear many hats each day not only as principal but as a father who is involved in his kids' lives. When I leave my school each day, the second half of my day is just beginning. I go home and have dinner with my family, talk about their day and become involved with all of them. The best thing I ever did was create a shared calendar with Google calendar. I share my professional calendar with my kids and my wife so that they understand how hard I work and how much I appreciate their understanding and support.[9] (T.J. Ebert, Principal)
- STRESS—To eliminate confusion and reduce stress in my day-to-day in-person and telephone encounters, I developed a system to organize what could be an overwhelming task. The best idea I ever had was to keep a spiral steno notepad in my office. I divided it into columns: date, time, name, request, person's contact info., disposition. I recorded every person's name (last name first) who came into the office or called on the phone to see or talk to me. This included other administrators, teachers and staff, parents,

and/or community members. I took notes when I spoke or shortly thereafter when things were fresh in my mind. I also used the last column, disposition, to indicate what I did as to the request. This provided me with a chronological list of contacts and requests. If I received another call or question about the request, I had a written record of what I did in response. I would also use a highlighter to indicate any difficult situations to alert myself for future encounters with the person. I used these notebooks as a history of my interactions and actions. I went through many notebooks each year but had a written record to fall back on. I even referred to old notebooks to provide a year-to-year history of encounters.[10] (D. Howell, Principal)

IDEAS FROM THE FIELD OF EDUCATIONAL ADMINISTRATION
OUTSIDE THE BOX THINKING
CHAPTER TWO—OTHERS

The second topic, Others, provides a variety of subjects and checklists to enable the building leader to interact with individuals and groups inside and outside the school. The ideas submitted by the administrators in the field focus on the need for communication to all stakeholders to promote a healthy school climate. Of special interest is the emphasis by these school leaders on the need to assume the role of instructional leader.

- COMMUNICATIONS—Below are the ways in which I communicated with all stakeholders regularly. I feel that an administrator should never assume that something is understood!

  Staff
  - Send a memo every Sunday evening—staff shout-outs, reminders, important dates, resources of the week, and quotes of the week are some pieces.
  - Staff Google folder—this housed anything ever sent to the staff via email, staff meetings, presentations, instructional handouts, and resources.

  Families
  - Twitter—Follow us @ ABC Elementary
  - Daily—Our fourth Grade students create daily video announcements.
  - Weekly—A weekly update will be sent home via School Connects to your email address in PowerSchool.
  - Weekly—Each teacher or grade level will send home a weekly newsletter or communication to parents.

- Monthly—The "ABC School Messenger" is sent home on the first school day of the month via School Connects to your email address in PowerSchool.[11] (A. Mcglenn, Principal)
- COMMUNICATIONS—I have found it useful to provide a framework that somewhat scripts parent–teacher conferences. Often, teachers are restricted by the time they must speak with families. I have worked within schools where conferences must fit within a time window of under 15 minutes. In my experience, this has been coupled with a lack of adequate preparation time for teachers ahead of conferences. This has led to rushed and staggered conversations where time runs out too quickly without being able to touch on all the points necessary. There is a lot to get through—attendance, class participation, performance on testing, etc. I have found that having teachers prepare their communication in this framework to be highly effective at keeping a conference targeted and thorough. See *Table D.3, Improving Communications, in appendix D*. As a bonus, we have printed these to supply to parents as a summary once conferences are completed—we have sent them home with interim reports and report cards. This is true even for those parents that have not participated in conferences.[12] (J. McHugh, Principal)
- COMMUNITY RELATIONS—Use the resources within your community to enhance what the students are learning. That does not always mean asking for donations. Ask a local landscaper or greenhouse to come in and talk about local/regional horticulture, invite your local historical society or library to come in and talk about your town's history, have a small business come in and talk about how to start a small business, etc. Some places might be close enough for a walking field trip where you can support local establishments for lunch and the students can learn about their community. Invite the community into your school and encourage your teachers and students to be active in their community.[13] (M. Sedlak, Principal)
- INSTRUCTIONAL LEADER—Some teachers have traditionally used lecture or teacher-directed instruction. To change instruction for the benefit of the learner, it is a rethinking of how lessons are presented and who is responsible for the learning. Some teachers may be uncomfortable with a change, so as the instructional leader, you must lead. Find resources, time, and experts to help you work with teachers. All efforts benefit the students and the learning.[14] (D. Howell, Principal)
- INSTRUCTIONAL LEADER—Becoming a strong instructional leader involves a three (3) to four (4) year process. Schools have so many moving parts that focusing on enhancing instruction cannot be an afterthought. Strengthening instruction and effectively leading your school through that must be a priority and a goal especially for a new principal.[15] (L. Teringo, Principal)

- INSTRUCTIONAL LEADER—During the day we have a 30-minute WIN (What I Need) period. Teachers divide the students within their grade level to make small groups (using support staff) to focus on individual needs. On Fridays, students set goals for themselves. The goals can be academic, behavioral, or organizational. Then, as a class, they come to the office to ring the bell if they have reached their goal. We have New Year's horns and noisemakers to really pump them up. Not all of them get to do it, but they still cheer for one another and motivate each other to meet their goal for the next week. There is no greater joy than to hear a child in January say, "This is my first time getting to ring the bell!" Or to watch another child clap for his friends who are shouting, "Oh yeah! Oh yeah!" Their excitement is invigorating! We have taught them that hard work and perseverance pay off.[16] (L. Stark, Principal)
- INSTRUCTIONAL LEADERSHIP—As a principal, use the framework below while implementing a schoolwide project:
  - Embrace and support teacher-initiated ideas and projects.
  - Foster and develop shared leadership and teacher-leader capacity.
  - Rally school-wide interest and excitement.
  - Encourage student involvement.
  - Be an active member of the project.
  - Find meaningful connections for staff/students.
  - Make learning come alive for students.[17] (J. Filomena, Principal)
- PROMOTING A HEALTHY ORGANIZATION—When developing our commitments and core beliefs for our school mission statement, we started with ideas and phrases and then created a word splash. Then the tweaking and wordsmithing process. The process took several meetings. Lots of time spent with buy-in from the teachers. They need to be part of the solution, so action plans are not viewed as one more thing. Each year we review and revise so that we keep current with educational changes and teacher changes. See *Elementary Mission Table D.4 in appendix D*.[18] (E. Tonello, Assistant Principal)
- SCHOOL CLIMATE—One of the best "management styles" I have ever witnessed or utilized has also been the simplest. You need to be in the hallways of your building. Management by Wandering Around (MBWA) allows you to interact with students and staff and gets you out of the office. You cannot run a school from behind a desk. I would also carry a small pad of paper with me and a pen for when a student or staff member would approach me with an issue or concern. Sometimes it was as simple as needing a light replaced. . . . . . . write it down and get it taken care of! You will learn more about your school population and climate by being in the hallways. Do not wait for the problems to come to you. . . . . . . by then, they have already been discussed.[19] (K. Baker, Director)

IDEAS FROM THE FIELD
OF EDUCATIONAL ADMINISTRATION
OUTSIDE THE BOX THINKING
CHAPTER THREE—ORGANIZATION

The chapter on Organization presents valid points to assist principals in developing organizational systems for dealing with special education, student activities, school-wide discipline policies, and student and staff recognition. Entries from practicing or former administrators echo the need for organization especially in the preparation for the start of school to guarantee a successful year.

- EXTRACURRICULAR ACTIVITIES—An assembly can be held for all clubs, music and drama groups, and athletics. Sponsors would have the opportunity to "sell" their activity to students. After the assembly, coaches, sponsors, and student participants would be housed at various tables in the cafeteria. This would allow for questions/answers and the opportunity to sell the sport or activity to other students. This creates enthusiasm for the activity and puts a face to the name of advisors and coaches.[20] (A. Anderson, Principal)
- EXTRACURRICULAR ACTIVITIES—Athletics and Extra-Curricular Activities within a school district is a wonderful opportunity for administrators to help support and enforce the idea of educational-based programming. Through these shared experiences with our coaches, advisors, and students, this concept is to help build well-rounded students that are preparing to enter the global workforce. Administrators can help support these programs through participation and attendance.

    Seek the activity students out during the school day to inquire as to how their activity is doing, what help and support do they need to have further success and the fact that we as a school, are all proud of your accomplishments and commitments to your activity. We look for ways that our students can help lead and be ambassadors to our school district, and this is a wonderful way to showcase the many talents of our students in a way that celebrities student success stories, on and off their fields of play or activity areas.[21] (R. Coxon, Assistant Principal)
- GETTING READY FOR SCHOOL—One of the most important pieces for starting the school year is preparing your support staff. Cooks, custodians, secretaries, aides, bus drivers, night custodians, and supervisory personnel are all essential to the successful start of a school year. Take time to meet with them as a group and individually to be sure they share your school philosophy and understand expectations, practices, and procedures. We invited all the bus drivers into the school for breakfast so we could be more collegial.[22] (A. Anderson, Principal)

- GETTING READY FOR SCHOOL—Establish the work to be accomplished in the spring and monitor it thru the summer. Maintenance, professional development, hires, etc. Do not disappear for three months and expect it to be ready.[23] (L. Bontempo, Principal)
- GETTING READY FOR SCHOOL—Using the summer months to prepare for the new school year is always my favorite time of the school year. One way my school gets ready for school is through various administrative meetings. We discuss culture, climate, instruction, and discipline. This year, we created a google document where we highlighted the strengths of each for the previous school year, listed goals for the new school year, and then created a plan to reach those goals. Another way I prepare for school is by focusing on my staff. Each summer I reach out to all staff to talk about what worked the previous year and ask them what they need to be more successful moving forward. I also involve staff in the professional development planning and delivery.[24] (H. Mueller, Principal)
- GETTING READY FOR SCHOOL—As we closed each school year in June, the Guidance Counselors and Administrators would meet to review their tasks and look ahead to the next school year. The guidance team of four counselors looped with their students. (Each counselor stayed with their students for four (4) years until graduation.) The Guidance Responsibility Chart was edited every August to align grade-level specific tasks with each grade-level counselor and administrator. *See Guidance Department Overview, Table D.5 in appendix D*. In addition to positive relationships being forged between a student and guidance counselor, solid relationships were often established between the administrator and guidance counselor, as students graduating in their caseload became their number one priority. Students were no longer "lost in the shuffle" of a large comprehensive high school.

   It is important to recognize that the goal to align counselors with grade-level administrators and depart from the alphabetical caseload model established years ago was not a smooth transition. Guidance counselors were very reluctant to transition to the grade-level model—especially when overseeing Seniors. Also, as we worked with this model for almost ten years, we accommodated parent requests who may have had concerns with a particular grade-level counselor and requested a switch or change to another counselor. The graduation "files" and student course history information always stayed with the grade-level counselor. But a student was always permitted to visit with a counselor he or she felt more comfortable with throughout their four years.[25] (L. Teringo, Principal)
- SPECIAL EDUCATION—Be an advocate for your special education students and urge your teachers to do the same. Do not forget about your at-risk or special needs students and the staff that works with those students.

A special education representative must have a seat on your BLT (Building Leadership Team)! District-level pupil services and the special education department in your building can assist you with enhancing co-teaching/inclusion strategies. Focusing on "pushing students in" to the general education setting with content teachers will strengthen instruction throughout your building.[26] (J. Teringo, Principal)

- STUDENT DISCIPLINE—While student discipline can be unpleasant and unpredictable, it can also create relationships with students that you would otherwise not have. Some of my most lasting relationships have been with "frequent flyers" to my office. The absolute key to creating the building climate you desire is to have a solid code of conduct (legally and applicable) and then to CONSISTENTLY apply the code to ALL students. As soon as you differentiate your discipline, it will usurp your position in the building. Students respect boundaries, and their inclination is to push that boundary as far as allowed. They will respect you if you are consistent, creating the building climate for effective learning.[27] (K. Baker, Director)
- STUDENT DISCIPLINE—Proximity Contract- While this does not technically fall under "discipline," it allows students to come together and sign a contract that stipulates they will not talk about the other person or approach the other person in the hallway until the issues have been resolved. It is signed by all the students involved and is kept on file to show progressive discipline and let the students know they are being watched closely when it comes to their behavior. Once issues are resolved, students come together and initial the contract to show they no longer need it, however, it is kept on file. *See Proximity Contract, Figure D.6, in appendix D.*[28] (E. Butler, Principal)
- STUDENT DISCIPLINE—Reentry Meeting—When a student is suspended, they are brought back under the assumption that the suspension or expulsion has enabled them to "learn their lesson." I have found that these behaviors are often repeated because the student may not quite understand that what they are doing is wrong, or they see the punishment as an intrinsic "reward" to get out of school. I like to make an emphasis on a suspension or expulsion by bringing the student in for a re-entry meeting. I stipulate in the suspension paperwork that the student cannot attend their classes until they meet with a principal to discuss what the original behavior was and come up with two measurable goals to prevent future behaviors from occurring.[29] (E. Butler, Principal)
- STUDENT DISCIPLINE—My philosophy regarding handling or managing student discipline for both teachers and administrators is based on multiple components. First, teachers and administrators should examine themselves to determine whether they themselves are the root cause of student misbehaviors or the lack of adherence to policies and regulations.

Oftentimes, both teachers and administrators bring personal attitudes, behaviors, biases, and previous negative experiences to school that they project upon students. Teachers and administrators should always be aware as to whether they have contributed to the negative behaviors of students.

Next, teachers and administrators should examine the policies that have been violated by students. What is the intention of the policy? Do the policies violate any student's rights? Are the policies equitably enforced across the entire student body regardless of gender, sexual orientation, race, ethnicity, religion, or parent influence?

Finally, has the student body had the opportunity to have joint ownership of the policies when appropriate? Do students have a voice in policy development and implementation when appropriate? Does the policy allow for the student body to play a role in self-governance when appropriate?[30] (F. Hampton, Associate Professor)

- STUDENT POSITIVE RECOGNITION—We take a "team" approach instead of individual awards or recognition, every classroom has a copy of the children's version of *How Full is Your Bucket?*[31] Teachers read it and discuss what it means to be a bucket filler. Each class has a bucket and tons of different sizes and color pom-poms. They must work together to demonstrate being responsible, respectful, kind/caring, and safe. The only way they can earn a "warm fuzzy" (pom-pom) is by earning a compliment from someone other than their teacher. When they fill a bucket, they bring it to me, and we make a big deal of it on the morning announcements. Then, I visit the class, give them stickers, and the teacher will offer them a class reward (pajama day, extra recess, popcorn party).[32] (L. Villa, Principal)

IDEAS FROM THE FIELD
OF EDUCATIONAL ADMINISTRATION
OUT OF THE BOX THINKING
CHAPTER FOUR—OPERATIONS

Operations is the fourth topic dealing with utilizing all the content presented in the first three topics to prepare the principal for dealing with the day-to-day workings of the school. The entries included from the field present ideas for the support of personnel management, budgeting, and the use of technology to improve the operations of the school.

- BUDGETING AND FINANCE—Get to know the treasurer, build a relationship of trust and open dialogue. Ask him/her for help and understanding of the fiscal process. Big budget mistakes will create major problems for leadership. Before you head down the path of new programming, have a planning discussion about the potential costs and budgets.[33] (B. Bontempo, Superintendent)

- BUDGETING AND FINANCE—This is complicated so working with district leadership to understand the budget process and funds available is important. During the year, keep a list of needs that you observe and report those to your supervisor. So much of the expenditures already have budgets established. The only way for your priorities to be met is to communicate those to your supervisors/superintendent/treasurer.

  As a principal, I utilized hanging file folders (in addition to online file folders) for all areas under my supervision, especially budgeting. These file folders hung in my desk drawer and were labeled for easy access for any meetings or responsibilities I had. Each week I met with my secretary and reviewed expenditures for the week, keeping notes and supportive documents in the binder. This gave me a written record if I needed to check with the treasurer's office.[34] (L. Bontempo, Principal)

- PERSONNEL MANAGEMENT—I believe it is important for me to help teachers "keep the main thing, the main thing." I want them to be able to focus on teaching and learning and improving their craft as a teacher daily. Minimizing teacher stress is crucial for teachers to focus on what is most important. Addressing small things that make a big difference helps with keeping the mind of teachers focused on their practice and the goals of the building clear. Not allowing distractions that get in the way of school improvement goals is key to success. I like to think of it as quick wins.

  Quick wins involve addressing barriers or conditions that require big or small moves that will make bold statements. For instance, at the start of my principalship in a new building I learn about what building conditions can be improved, school improvement practices, organizational procedures and routines, and traditions or practices that cause teachers the most stress. I then begin to outline a plan to address these issues and this gives teachers the opportunity to see that I have the ability and skills to implement change. When teachers see things changing and conditions improving, it creates a momentum that everyone wants to take part in.[35] (A. Harper, Principal)

- PERSONNEL MANAGEMENT—While at my last district, our administrative team led by our superintendent focused on making great hires for the district. In many ways hiring employees is a business investment decision.

  We must look at each hire as an investment. A huge investment that will likely be on the books for years to come, sometimes a career. Removing an ineffective employee can be done over time, maybe years, however, it is an arduous process. Taking the time during the hiring process will make a big difference for the school district over time.

Thorough interviewing followed by a practical demonstration of skills is necessary to the process of making a good investment in your school's future. To round out the hiring process, a rigorous reference check should be completed. Not only supplied references should be checked, but three-four non-supplied references. Our interview team would brainstorm on how to determine non-supplied references and make the calls.[36] (J. Teringo, Principal)

- SAFETY AND SECURITY—Safety is an essential part of the school. Be sure to stay current on new laws, regulations governing the safety of schools. When it comes to the safety and security of your students and staff, include your local first responders at every step of the planning process. Invite them into your building as often as possible. Introduce them to the staff, students, and families. Make them a part of your culture. The first time you meet your first responders, and they enter your building should not be during an active crisis.[37] (M. Sedlak, Principal)
- TECHNOLOGY—Technology is necessary for schools today. It can prove to be a major asset for your school and for you. It is impossible for the principal to stay current and to meet the needs of a changing school program. Take time to compile a committee of resource persons (both in the school and in the community) who can advise you on new hardware and software for the students and teachers and for you as well.[38] (A. Harper, principal)
- TECHNOLOGY—I have found using Google Classrooms to be an effective way to manage deliverables for teachers. This is great at the start of the year for the various signatures needed and compliance pieces, like the staff handbook, to disseminate. It is set up exactly the same way as it would be for students, using the "topics" function to break down by department or theme (i.e., TBT, OTES, Sign-in, etc.). It proves particularly effective for sharing school-specific handbooks, reference materials.

  Another aspect I favor is the "to do" function that keeps deadlines organized for staff. I always give ample time during any staff meeting for educators to consult their "to do" items and complete anything outstanding. Essentially, any materials or action items for teachers can be funneled through Classrooms.[39] (J. McHugh, Principal)
- TECHNOLOGY—As many districts focused on virtual learning and hybrid models of instruction, the principal had to examine the virtual learning strengths of staff members. We collectively determined a different focus for instruction. I asked the teachers to create in-house mini "how to videos" that were shared with the staff. We have had so much newness affecting the instruction of our students but knowing that there was someone on campus that was an accessible "expert" helped to build momentum. This created synergy and collaboration. The staff began to develop a sense of belonging

and were able to connect and communicate with each other for help. The social–emotional connections of the staff aided the movement and changes in instructional behavior. With teaching staff on board, the end goal was for the students to have engaging lessons for both traditional and virtual learning.[40] (E. Tonello, Assistant Principal)

- TECHNOLOGY—The last Wednesday of every month we created "Winning Wednesdays," in that if a teacher's door was open on these days that meant your room is fair game for any staff member to walk in and see the happenings of the room. These days teachers are encouraged to look at classroom management skills, technology ideas, best practices, etc. With the spirit of "Winning Wednesdays," we would finalize those days with the Podcast crew. A week before the day I would send out a motivational/educational podcast for all to listen to. We would meet at the end of Winning Wednesdays and discuss the day and discuss the Podcast and the relatability for our school climate and culture. (J. Vanek, Middle School Principal)[41]

CHAPTER FIVE—CONCLUSION

Developing Outside Networks and Gaining Effective Practices for Inside-the-School Success

The content for chapter 5 was included to provide a culmination to the entire book, *Creating an Award-Winning School: Outside the Box Thinking for Inside-the-School-Success*. The authors felt that the topic of Outreach was essential to examine as it constitutes an important part of the position of the principal of any school. To be a successful school administrator at any grade level or in any district, the leader must have the confidence to reach out to peers, community members, associates, and persons of support. Developing a circle of mentors and others in key positions can help the building leader as they understand the scope and responsibilities of the role.

Carefully selecting former colleagues, professors, community members, and fellow district administrators can create a valuable network to serve as a vital connection for the school leader. In turn, the building leader can self-analyze his/her own attributes to determine what can be offered to the members of the network. An additional outreach avenue is provided by the state, regional or national administrative organizations who have conferences, workshops, websites, and publications to enhance personal and professional knowledge. The leader must be confident and willing to make the connections that can benefit him or her and the school as well.

As a part of this last chapter, the authors included ideas from current and past administrators that have been part of the authors' own networks. Ideas were selected from a variety of male and female, current and former principals in all grade levels to highlight valuable concepts that have become tried and true techniques implemented in the field.

Key concepts from chapter 5 include:

- Take time to self-evaluate, analyze interruptions and events that may be causing your stress. You may be able to eliminate some of the stress by self-reflecting.
- Embrace and support teacher-initiated ideas and projects by fostering and developing shared leadership.
- Becoming a strong instructional leader involves a three-to-four-year process. Strengthening instruction and effectively leading your school through that must be a priority.
- Be an advocate for your special education students and urge your teachers to do the same.
- Make an emphasis on reentry meetings following a suspension or expulsion.
- It takes all of us to build and maintain a positive school climate.

As the reader finishes chapter 5, it could be a time to contemplate the development of a network by reaching out to the role models from the past and present to help in guiding the leader to a successful future as a building principal.

INSIDE-THE-SCHOOL SUCCESS
READER'S THOUGHTS ON THE CHECKLIST

Reflection is an important part of being a leader. Following your reading, take time to assess the information and consider its meaning and usefulness to you as a principal. Before moving on to the next topic, take time to reflect on the topics you just completed. After reviewing the lists and the supportive materials, choose at least two items and explain how you would use them in your leadership role to ensure school success and Create an Award-Winning School.

_____
_____
_____
_____

Review the *Outside the Box Thinking* included after the checklists or in the appendix to determine how you might use a technique now or in the future in your leadership role. Place your thoughts below on how you may implement this technique or how you might alter the technique to suit your role as a leader.

_____
_____
_____
_____
_____

Be sure to save your thoughts on this topic for future reference. Try to share something new with a colleague or staff member.

NOTES

1. T.J. Ebert, Elementary Principal, Independence Local Schools, *Goal Setting*, November 2020.

2. Amey Mcglenn, Elementary Principal, Marysville Exempted Village Schools, *Goal Setting*, October 2020.

3. Haley Mueller, Elementary Principal, Northeast Ohio College Preparatory School, *Goal Setting*, November 2020.

4. Brian Bontempo, Superintendent, Auburn Career Center, *Personal Behavior*, November 2020.

5. Deborah Morin, Director, Center for Educational Leadership, Cleveland State University, *Personal Behavior*, December 2020.

6. Rob Coxon, Assistant Principal, Olmstead Falls, *Personal Behavior*, December 2020.

7. Lynne Stark, Elementary Principal, Clearview Local Schools, *Problem Solving*, October 2020.

8. Jennifer E. Filomena, Elementary Principal, Hudson City Schools, *Stress*, October 2020.

9. T.J. Ebert, Elementary Principal, Independence Local Schools, *Stress*, October 2020.

10. Deb Howell, High School Principal, Medina City Schools, *Stress*, September 2020.

11. Amey Mcglenn, Elementary Principal, Marysville Exempted Village Schools, *Communications*, October 2020.

12. Jordan McHugh, Principal, Constellation Schools, *Communications*, November 2020.

13. Michael J. Sedlak, Intermediate Principal, Hudson City Schools, *Community Relations*, September 2020.

14. Deb Howell, High School Principal, Medina City Schools, *Instructional Leadership*, October 2020.

15. Louise Teringo, High School Principal, Twinsburg City Schools, *Instructional Leadership,* December 2020.
16. Lynne Stark, Elementary Principal, Clearview Local Schools, *Instructional Leadership,* November 2020.
17. Jennifer E. Filomena, Elementary Principal, Hudson City Schools, *Instructional Leadership*, October 2020.
18. Erika Tonello, Assistant Principal, Pasco County Schools, *Promoting a Healthy Organization,* September 2020.
19. Kenneth Baker, former Executive Director, Ohio Association of Secondary School Principals, *School Climate*, November 2020.
20. Andrea Anderson, Middle School Principal, Oak Lawn Schools, *Extra Curricular Activities*, September 2020.
21. Rob Coxon, Assistant Principal, Olmstead Falls, *Extra Curricular Activities*, December 2020.
22. Andrea Anderson, Middle School Principal, Oak Lawn Schools, *Getting Ready for School*, September 2020.
23. Lisa Bontempo, Assistant High School Principal, Hudson City Schools, *Getting Ready for School*, December 2020.
24. Haley Mueller, Elementary Principal, Northeast Ohio College Preparatory School, *Getting Ready for School*, December 2020.
25. Louise Teringo, High School Principal, Twinsburg City Schools, *Getting Ready for School,* November 2020.
26. Jeff Teringo, Assistant High School Principal, Wadsworth City Schools, *Special Education,* November 2020.
27. Kenneth Baker, former Executive Director, Ohio Association of Secondary School Principals, *Student Discipline,* December 2020.
28. Eric Butler, Assistant Principal, Ashtabula Area City Schools, *Student Discipline,* November 2020.
29. Eric Butler, Assistant Principal, Ashtabula Area City Schools, *Student Discipline,* November 2020.
30. Fred Hampton, Associate Professor of Educational Administration, *Student Discipline,* December 2020.
31. Rath, Tom and Mary Reckmeyer. *How Full is Your Bucket for Kids.* Washington D.C.: Gallup Press, 2009.
32. Lynn Villa, Elementary Principal, Twinsburg City Schools, *Student Positive Recognition,* November 2019.
33. Brian Bontempo, Superintendent, Auburn Career Center, *Budgeting and Finance,* December 2020.
34. Lisa Bontempo, Assistant High School Principal, Hudson City Schools, *Budgeting and Finance*, December 2020.
35. Angela Harper, Elementary Principal, Akron Public Schools, *Personnel Management*, November 2020.
36. Jeff Teringo, Assistant High School Principal, Wadsworth City Schools, *Personnel Management,* December 2020.
37. Michael J. Sedlak, Intermediate Principal, Hudson City Schools, *Safety and Security,* October 2020.

38. Angela Harper, Elementary Principal, Akron Public Schools, *Technology*, November 2020.

39. Jordan McHugh, Principal, Constellation Schools, *Technology*, December 2020.

40. Erika Tonello, Assistant Elementary Principal, Pasco County Schools, *Technology*, October 2020.

41. Jamie Vanek, Middle School Principal, Independence Local Schools, *Technology*, December 2020.

Conclusion

The authors have written the conclusion to the book as a reflection of their own careers in educational administration. While relaying their history of experiences, they have highlighted key concepts from the text that were important to each of them in their leadership roles.

BEING A PRINCIPAL

A Reflection by Dr. Janet M. Litzel

Being an Elementary Principal

I had been teaching in the elementary school for six years when I returned to earn my Master's degree in Elementary Administration. I did not immediately pursue a position because I was coaching and had a young child and had moved to the middle school as a teacher. When the principalship opened in the elementary school in which I had previously taught, I was encouraged to apply. After three separate interviews, I earned the position and returned to the school that I had taught in for twelve years. So, I remained in the same school district and became the leader of a K-4 building. I was initially a bit overwhelmed as I was the only principal, but I tried to rely on the people who had been there before me for advice. Our district was realigning, and my school had increased from 170 students to 493 students and the staff tripled in size through the summer that I took over. *I learned quickly that a positive school climate was a major challenge and that I needed the entire staff and student body to work together to create one.*

The hardest thing was to arrange the school for new students and staff in a short period of time. I had no assistant principal or counselors, so I became fast friends and coworkers with the custodian and secretary. *The implementation of a problem-solving model was essential to assist me in developing sound decisions making practices.*

The best part of my first position was working with the students and staff. *I relied on the expertise of my staff in implementing an Intervention Assistance Team to better meet the needs of our special education students.* We were truly able to make a collaborative community school while I was there. After four years at the elementary school, I applied to move to the same middle school in which I had taught, being the first female principal there.

Being a Middle School Principal

Moving to middle school was a major change for me. I was tasked with making the school follow the model of Ohio middle schools with teaching teams and collaborative instruction. The school was a 7–8 grade configuration with 320 students. *Since I was the only principal in the building, I looked forward to working with the staff to establish consistent room rules, behavioral expectations, and a school-wide discipline plan.* Half of the students attending the middle school had been in my elementary when I was a principal there so that was an advantage. I also had taught with most of the teachers in the building and knew the support staff. I was excited about middle school because I really enjoyed teaching sixth and eighth grade when I was there before. *It was at this position that I began to focus and work to become the instructional leader of the school.*

The hardest thing was the physical facilities. Half of the school built in 1920 was closed so that all classes and activities were held in the other half of the building, which was built in 1950. *School climate became an emphasis as we worked together to improve the school facilities for safety and security.*

The best thing about being at the middle school was the students. It was powerful to see the changes in students I had known since they were in kindergarten. It was also a great experience working with the teachers to implement teaming and improving instruction. During that time, we were able to collectively pass a construction levy and replace the old 1920 wing with a new one while renovating the 1950s section. There was never a dull moment for sure.

Moving to a New District

After four years, construction, and middle school implementation, I was asked to interview at another district to become a sixth, seventh, and eighth grade principal. The goal was to create teams, and a middle school schedule (sound familiar?). After a series of round table interviews which included students, I was asked to join a new school of 360 students and a staff of 40. I was excited at the opportunity to begin a newly configured middle school because I had two counselors, a psychologist, and two secretaries, who were supportive, and an energetic staff but no assistant principal. *This was an important time for me in that I had to learn a new contract language, hiring, evaluations, and mentoring practices for a new district.*

The hardest thing for me was that I had had the advantage of being in the same district for twenty-four years and was now learning people and places all over again. The best thing was that all the staff was eager for change and the administration supported the changes, too.

After two years at this new district, I had an opportunity to move into teaching in higher education. I had been an adjunct graduate instructor for six years after earning my doctorate in educational administration. *Relying on my reflective practices, goal setting, and personal mission statement*, I determined that moving to the university level would provide me with an opportunity to affect change in undergraduate and graduate education students.

At the university, I was able to rely on the skills as an instructional leader as my responsibilities were in teaching undergraduate and graduate teacher and principal candidates. Later my position expanded to an administrative one as I became a director in the student teaching program. Depending on my leadership skills again I worked closely with hundreds of students, supervisors, area school leaders, and college personnel. I discovered that many leadership competencies such as communications, personnel management, community relations, instructional leadership that were used as a building principal transcended my role in higher education.

I really enjoyed and appreciated my years as an elementary and middle school principal as they provided me a solid foundation for university teaching and a *network of resources* in the field. The university afforded me the opportunity to truly develop as a *network of resources* in the field. Being in administration followed me to the university level as I later became director of student teaching.

As a principal, I grew as an educator having the opportunity to view students learning in a variety of settings. I think the most important thing about the principal's position is that you have an opportunity to affect change in students, parents, teachers, and staff that can last them a lifetime. It is really a powerful position for an educator.

BEING A PRINCIPAL

A Reflection by Dr. Joanie A. Walker

Being an Assistant Principal

I had been teaching at the high school level for seven years when I returned to earn my Master's degree in Secondary Administration. I decided I wanted to become a school administrator because I wanted to have a bigger influence on the overall school climate and culture. After earning my master's degree in Secondary Administration two years later and with nine years' experience as a high school teacher, I pursued my first high school assistant principal position.

It was difficult to obtain my first high school principal job as a female because over 95% of high school administrators were male at the time. Administrators where I was teaching even encouraged me to apply for an elementary or middle school administrator job since it "might be easier to obtain as a female." My desire was to obtain a high school level administrator's job since all my teaching and coaching experience was at the high school. After interviewing with several districts, I was finally hired as an Assistant Principal at a township school district an hour drive from my house.

As the new Assistant Principal, I was assigned the eleventh and twelfth graders for student management and discipline. Other duties included: teacher observations and evaluations, coordination of assemblies, academic awards, and graduation. District duties included serving as the district coordinator for proficiency testing as well as serving on the strategic planning technology committee.

The hardest part of my job was aligning discipline expectations with fellow administrators that had different leadership style and philosophies. Sometimes after I would assign a discipline consequence according to our student code of conduct, the student would run to another administrator and they would overturn it. This made it difficult to be fair and consistent among our student body when it came to student discipline. Something I told myself was once I became a principal, I would be fair and consistent with student discipline and more importantly, support my assistant principal's decisions.

The best part of the role as an assistant principal was the daily contact with the students. I enjoyed supervising sports and activities by getting to see the students perform outside of the classroom. I also enjoyed assisting with awards programs and graduation and witnessing the student's growth and accomplishments. *To support a positive school climate, it is important to acknowledge students' accomplishments in several ways.*

Being a Unit Principal

After serving two years as a high school assistant principal, I was fortunate to be hired as a Unit Principal at the largest high school in Ohio. As a Unit Principal, we would move with our grade level until they graduated and start over again with the incoming tenth graders. Each grade level consisted of a total of 950 students. I served in the role of a Unit Principal for six years, seeing two classes through to graduation. Each Unit had a Unit Principal, three guidance counselors, and one secretary. The purpose of the Unit was to create "a school within a school concept." *In this position, I created the student discipline grid so that our three-unit principals were consistent and fair with discipline.*

As a Unit Principal, my duties included: Student discipline of 950 students, oversaw Individualized Educational Plans (IEP) for 100 students, coordinated grade level newsletters, academic awards, student activities and assemblies, awards programs, graduation, and teacher observations and evaluations for fifty teachers. District duties included: Facilitator of the Building Level Technology Committee and Secondary Curriculum Liaison for the Business Department (Jr. High and High School).

The hardest part of serving as a Unit Principal was the number of discipline referrals received for 950 students, sometimes 50 referrals a day. The best part was the daily interaction with students for reasons other than discipline. *Students don't always take the time to say thank you when we support their activities, but when we don't support them or are not visible, they are quick to point it out illustrating how important recognition is.* The position of Unit Principal provided me with great experience as I prepared for my first principal position.

After serving two years as a high school Assistant Principal and six years as a Unit Principal, I was ready to apply for my first head high school principal job. The other factor of preparedness for a head principal job was that I had completed my Doctorate in Educational Administration and my three children were older.

Being a High School Principal

The same thing occurred when I applied for my first Assistant Principal job; it was difficult as a female to be hired as a high school principal. In fact, during a final interview, a superintendent told me that "I didn't look tough enough to be a principal." After applying for several principal positions, I was finally offered my first head principal job at an urban high school that had 1,300 students, four assistant principals, one athletic director, and four guidance counselors. I served in that role for four years.

As the high school principal, some of my duties included: organized and managed the high school and/or departments; faculty, staff, and administrative observations and evaluations; developed and implemented progressive curriculum changes; responsible for student management and school safety; collaborated with the athletic director regarding student activities; and developed and implemented building technology plan. District duties included: served on the District Professional Learning Communities Committee and the District Safety and Security Committee.

The best part of the job was I was hired as a change agent and was able to make the necessary changes to improve our school. My teachers were hard-working, and my students embraced the idea of school improvement as they too wanted a better school climate and culture. *I organized a student leadership group that I considered to be my "board of directors," who had a voice as to the activities and new ideas at our school.* I wanted to continue to learn and grow professionally so I accepted a new position.

My second and last high school principal job was at a suburban high school an hour's drive from my home, with 1,200 students, two assistant principals, one athletic director, and three guidance counselors. I held that position for nine years.

My duties at this school included: organize and manage school and/or departments; faculty, staff, and administrative evaluations; oversee student management and school safety; collaborate with the athletic director regarding student activities; development and implementation of building technology plan; manage building budget and physical resources. District duties included: District Coordinator for the Resident Educator Program and a member of the District Professional Evaluation Procedure Committee.

The best part of this job was the high school was already a great school, but our goal was to make it even better by updating our curriculum and programs. The teachers and students were hard-working with a supportive school community. The hardest part of the job was making the decision to leave after twenty-one years as a school administrator and pursue a career as a college professor. After spending thirty years working with high school students, to this day, I really miss the kids.

As a high school administrator, the early mornings along with averaging three to four nights per week can be demanding especially with three children. I had my children attend school events with me so that we could be together. My children would tease that they had more spirit wear clothes from the school I worked at than the school they attended. Although the hours were long, I always enjoyed being visible and available to students.

In both of my high school principal positions, I created the motto, *"It takes all of us to build and maintain a positive school climate."* Meaning, all students, parents, teachers, administrators, guidance counselors, custodians, and secretaries must work together on the same goals to build and maintain a positive school climate. This motto was visibly displayed in the cafeteria at both high schools I served as principal. The motto was also printed on student and staff t-shirts. During school assemblies, students knew what we stood for by easily reciting our school motto.

After thirty years of secondary education, I left the principalship to become a professor of practice at a large urban university. I currently teach for two educational leadership departments and I rely on my skills from my years as a school administrator. Some of these skills include communication, organization, stress management, student management, and personnel management.

Although I am not working directly with students as a college professor, I am indirectly helping them by teaching teachers to become future administrators.

I absolutely loved serving as a high school administrator. It was great getting to know and helping so many wonderful students, teachers, parents, and staff. Working with students was my favorite part of the job. It was a great educational experience to watch freshmen enter high school and grow into mature seniors graduating and moving onto the next phase of their lives. I also enjoyed working with teachers and watching them learn and grow as educators.

So how did this book come to be? Well, as we have emphasized throughout our text, principals have a need to develop a network and to reach out to people who have been an influence throughout their careers. This book is a direct result of the combined networks of both authors. As a building principal, Dr. Litzel served as an adjunct instructor in graduate studies at a major university when Dr. Walker took her first classes in educational administration. A friendship was forged, and both kept in touch as Dr. Walker began her principal positions. At the same time, Dr. Litzel retired from hers and moved to higher education to assume a full-time faculty position. While Dr. Walker served as a building leader, she continued to pursue her education. Later Dr. Litzel served on her dissertation committee when she received her doctoral degree.

As both moved in their separate careers, they continued to consult and meet on a variety of topics. When Dr. Walker retired from being a principal and moved to higher education, she contacted Dr. Litzel to accept a position teaching for the same university. It was then that the "wheels began to turn" and the idea of the book became more than a vision.

The book, *Creating an Award-Winning School*, is the result of the authors' networking over many years and sharing experiences and knowledge from a variety of schools, districts, and academic levels. Dr. Litzel and Dr. Walker are real-life examples of the benefit of networking and collaborating with administrators in the field.

Appendix A

My Compliments to You!

Dear _____

Please accept my compliments on _____
_____
_____
_____

Signed _____

NAME OF HIGH SCHOOL   FACULTY, STAFF & STUDENT COMPLIMENT CARD

Figure A.1. My Compliments to You

POSITIVE REFERRAL

Name: _____   Grade: _____

Counselor: _____   Date: _____

Check the appropriate box:

☐ Exemplary Behavior   ☐ Improved Behavior

☐ Exemplary Academic Achievement   ☐ Improved Academic Achievement

☐ Other:

_____
_____
_____
_____

Explanation: _____
_____
_____

Teacher: _____   Principal: _____

Figure A.2. Positive Referral Form

Committee Evaluation of School-Community Program

At the end of each semester, involve members of your staff and community in reflection. Take time to brainstorm and answer questions that help lead your school to the improvement of school and community interactions.

- How many connections were made within the school between teachers and staff in support of a positive school climate? List some examples.
- What connections were made between students in grade levels/subject areas and other students in support of a positive school climate? List some examples.
- How effective do you feel these new connections were?
  (rate them 1–10 with 1 being little effectiveness and 10 being long-lasting and enduring)?
- Why do you feel these programs are effective?

Some questions you could discuss for evaluation of outside community relationships could be:

- What connection/programs have been made between the school and the community to improve positive school-community relations?
- Who is involved in these programs and when are these occurring?
- Where are these programs held and how many students and staff and community members are involved?
- How effectively do you feel these programs are and why?

List any suggestions you might have to improve the interactions within and without of our school in our efforts to improve school-community relations.

Figure A.3. Committee Evaluation of School-Community Program

Appendix B

BEGINNING OF SCHOOL CHECKLIST
ADMINISTRATIVE TASKS

- Class meetings planned
- All forms printed and stacked for teacher distribution
- Manuals ready to distribute
- Rooms ready, cleaned, set up, assigned to staff
- Class lists printed/ Study Hall lists printed
- Code of Conduct posted throughout building and classrooms
- Homerooms assigned; rooms designated
- Schedules done, printed, ready to distribute
- Fair Share list printed for staff
- Key distribution ready for teachers/staff
- Emergency Instructions (Fire, Tornado, etc.) posted in classrooms and offices
- Student Handbooks/Planners printed and ready to distribute (also available online)
- Teacher packets ready for distribution
- Clocks synchronized, bells working
- Desks in each classroom (proper number)
- Lockers cleaned, locks inspected, and combinations changed
- Teacher workrooms set up and ready
- Sub-folders ready
- Staff mailboxes set up and ready
- Opening Teachers' Day Convocation planned
- First day of school schedule planned
- Teacher, Home Room & Principal's Letter to Staff & Principal Newsletter Checklist Completed
- Review of all items with Custodians, Secretaries, and administrative personnel

Figure B.1. Beginning of School Checklist

Appendix B

FACILITIES WALK THROUGH CHECKLIST

As a principal, it is advantageous to examine the physical facilities with your maintenance personnel at least once a week. A quick walk-through of your building can provide you with up-to-date information to ensure the safety and well-being of the students and staff. A checklist could help to give everyone a record of the condition of the facilities and any repairs that need to be made.

Facilities	Cleaning needed	Repairs Needed	Facilities	Cleaning needed	Repairs needed
Outside Walkways			Cafeteria/ Kitchen		
Inside Entrance			Gymnasium and Areas		
Office Areas and Hallways			Specialty Areas/ Labs/ Library/ Work Areas		
Boys' Restrooms			Classrooms: Doors, windows, furniture, flooring, room numbers		
Girls' Restrooms			Extra notes on cleaning and repairs		
Other Areas			Other Areas		

Figure B.2. Facilities Checklist

FACULTY MEETING

SAMPLE AGENDA

Welcome

General Business

A. Introductions
   1. New Faculty and Staff
   2. New Positions
B. School Resource Officer Information—Resource Officer
C. Changes
   1. Open Enrollment Health Insurance (Benefit Counselor)
   2. Evaluation Cycle and Student Growth Measures—House Bill 362
   3. Hunger Free Kids Act of 2010—No Bake Sales and Candy Sales (school day)
   4. Mass Casualty Evacuation Location
D. Expectations
   1. Professional Learning Communities
   2. It takes all of us to build and maintain a positive school climate
   3. Communication—"This and That" E-mail, Voicemail, Mailboxes
   4. Visibility and accountability—supervision in halls
   5. Chain of Command
   6. Special Education: IEP/504

Appendix B 121

      7. Sub Folders/Paperwork
      8. Class size, student schedule issues
      9. Online Calendar—Go Green—use of paper
     10. Electricity
     11. Field trips—Special approval after Spring Break
E. Instructional
      1. Open House
F. Staff Handbook
G. Miscellaneous
      1. Fire Department Inspection and Fire Drill
         • Inspection—October thru March
         • Microwaves, grills, heaters, obstruction of exits
      2. In-service Day
      3. Code Red—Phone numbers
H. Code of Conduct
      1. Progressive Discipline Plan
      2. Discipline referrals/procedures—Please read faculty/staff handbook
      3. Suspension Consequences
         1st = Credit given for work completed
         2nd = No make-up credit available except for Midterms & Exams
      4. Teacher assigned office detentions, cutting class
I. Student Supervision
      1. Never leave students unsupervised in your classroom
      2. Please assist with visibility by standing in your doorway during class changes
      3. Staff procedural outlines some more specific details of supervising students, especially for assemblies and study halls
      4. Please always assist with positive school climate by confronting inappropriate behavior
J. Staff Attendance
      1. Emergency lesson plans (sub folders)
      2. Procedure for obtaining a full day sub or period sub. Sub coverage form
K. Student Attendance
      1. Unexcused with credit
      2. Five- & seven-day notices (electronically), Loss of Credit
L. Physical Plant/Materials
      1. Keys
      2. Emergency Procedures
      3. Safety/Security—A.L.I.C.E. (one per year)—Emergency plan
M. Student Aides
      1. Procedure—Student accountability (first period)
      2. Supervision
O. Athletic Issues
      1. Athletic Code of Conduct
      2. Attendance at athletic events = on duty
      3. Weight Room
P. Other Issues, Questions and Concerns

Figure B.3. Faculty Meeting Sample Agenda

ADMINISTRATIVE RESPONSIBILITIES (Date of the current school year)

Principal

Instructional Leadership
- Business
- Guidance
- Language Arts
- Special Education
- Music

Coordination/Oversite
- Administrative Responsibilities
- Annual Discipline Report
- Building Budgets
- Business Contracts
- Classified Evaluations
- Commencement
- Communication (Press Releases)
- Curricular Initiatives
- Emergency Medical Forms
- Master Schedule
- Newsletter
- Open House
- Parent/Teacher Conferences
- Planned Absence
- PTA Council
- Public Relations Committee
- School Resource Officer
- Special Assignments
- Staff Scoop
- Student Accident Reports

Assistant Principal

Instructional Leadership
- Foreign Language
- Health/Physical Education
- Mathematics
- Science

Coordination/Oversite
- 10th and 11th Grade
  - Achievement
  - Activities
  - Attendance Issues
  - Discipline
- AAL
- Attendance/Year End Summary
- Bells/Clocks
- Building Permits/Facility Usage
- Classified Evaluations
- Class Size Report
- DAC
- Exam Coordinator
- Fair Share
- Grade/Interim Report
- Homeroom Lists
- ISACP Coordinator
- LPDC Representative
- Master Schedule-Data Entry Liaison
- Parent/Student Handbook
- Renaissance/Student Recognition

Assistant Principal

Instructional Leadership
- Art
- Media Center
- OWA/OWE
- Practical Studies
- Social Studies

Coordination/Oversite
- 9th and 12th Grade
  - Achievement
  - Activities
  - Attendance Issues
  - Discipline
- Activity Coordinator
- Alternative School Options
- Blood Mobile
- Building Maintenance
- Classified Evaluations
- Course Selection Guide
- Dances
- Disaster Crisis Manager
- Eighteen (18) Year Old Students
- Emergency Procedures (Drills)
- Evacuation Procedures
- Inventory (Physical/Textbook)
- LCJVS Liaison
- Master Schedule-Data Entry
- Message Boards

Athletic Director

Instructional Leadership
- Athletic Eligibility
- Assistant Coach Evaluation
- Coach Evaluation

Coordination/Oversite
- Athletic Boosters
- Athletic Code of Conduct
- Athletic Physicals
- Athletic Programs
- Budget Accounts
- Building Permits (Athletic, Recreational) /Facility Usage
- Scheduling
- Sports Medicine
- Supervision Schedule

Student Discipline Coordinator
Student Leaders
Student Teachers
Supervisory Schedules
Support Staff Procedural Manual
SWC
Teacher Checkout
Teacher Procedural Manual

Approval Agent
  Business Leave
  Field Trips
  Professional Leave
  Purchase Orders
  TV Requests
  Vacation

Room Utilization
SST 10th & 11th Grades
Student/Building Attendance
  Procedures
Student Lockers/Locks
Testing Coordinator
Work Permits

Assemblies
  Schedules
  Seating
  Supervision

Staff Attendance
  Emergency Coverage
  Report Forms
  Subs

School Pictures/Student ID
Security/Vandalism Reports
Senior Pass
Showcases
Spirit Week
SST 9th & 12th Grades
Student Fees
Student Parking
Technology Committee
Transition (Freshmen
  Orientation)
Vending/Phone

Figure B.4. Administrative Responsibilities Chart

NAME OF HIGH SCHOOL
DISCIPLINE CONSEQUENCES GRID (School Year)

01 Insubordination/Disrespect
- 1st Saturday School
- 2nd ISACP (1)
- 3rd OSS (1)
- 4th Rule #28 OSS (3)

02 Tardiness (per semester) AM to School
- 1st N/A
- 2nd N/A
- 3rd Detention (1)
- 4th Detention (2)
- 5th OPS (1)
- 6th Saturday School (1)
- 7th Saturday School (1)
- 8th ISACP (1)
- 9th ISACP (2)
- 10th ISACP (3)
- 11th ISACP (4)
- 12th OSS (1)
- 13th OSS (3)
- 14th OSS (5)

Tardy to Class (per semester)
- 1st Warning
- 2nd Detention (1)
- 3rd Detention (1)
- 4th and Above Office Referral

03 Class Cutting
- 1st OPS (1)
- 2nd Saturday School (1)

08 Distribution of Unauthorized Materials
- 1st Detention (1)
- 2nd Detention (2)
- 3rd Saturday School (1)

09 Inappropriate Appearance
(Time out of Class is Unexcused)
- 1st Warning and change of clothes
- 2nd Detention (1) and change of clothes
- 3rd OPS (1) and change of clothes
- 4th Saturday School (1) and change of clothes ISACP (1)
- 5th ISACP (3)
- 6th ISACP (5)
- 7th Rule #28 OSS (1, 3, 5, 10)

10 Electronic Devices
- 1st Warning. Students pick up device after school
- 2nd Saturday School (1) loss of device until parent pick up
- 3rd ISACP (1) loss of device until parent pick-up
- 4th ISACP (3)
- 5th ISACP (5)
- 6th Rule #28 OSS (1, 3, 5, 10)

11 Failure to Complete Detention
- 1st OPS (1)
- 2nd Saturday School (1)
- 3rd Saturday School (2)

16 Inappropriate Display of Affection
- 1st Detention (1)
- 2nd Detention (2)
- 3rd Saturday School (1)

17 Other Misconduct
- 1st Detention (1)
- 2nd Detention (2)
- 3rd Saturday School (1)

Café Other Misconduct
- 1st Saturday School (1)
- 2nd ISACP (1)
- 3rd ISACP (3)
- 4th ISACP (5)
- 5th Rule #28 OSS (1, 3, 5, 10)

SUSPENSIONS

18 Tobacco
(Separate from Rest of Progression)
- 1st OSS (3)
- 2nd OSS (6)
- 3rd OSS (10) with Recommendation for Expulsion

19 Gambling
- 1st Detention (1)
- 2nd Saturday School (1)
- 3rd ISACP (1)

3rd ISACP (3)
4th Rule #28 OSS (1, 3, 5, 10)

3rd Saturday School (2)
  4th ISACP (1)
  5th ISACP (3)
  6th OSS (3)
  7th OSS (5)

04 **Truancy**
  1st OPS (1)
  2nd Saturday School (1)
  3rd Saturday School (2)
  4th ISACP (1)
  5th ISACP (3)
  6th Rule #28 OSS (1, 3, 5, 10)

05 **Loitering**
  1st Detention (1)
  2nd Detention (2)
  3rd Saturday School (1)

06 **Minor Violations of Bus Code Requirements**
  Administrative Discretion

07 **Motor Vehicle Offenses**
  Administrative Discretion
  1st Detention (1)
  2nd Saturday School (1)
  3rd Saturday School (2)
  4th ISACP (1)
  5th ISACP (3)
  6th ISACP (5)
  7th Rule #28 OSS (1, 3, 5, 10)

  4th ISACP (1)
  5th ISACP (3)
  6th ISACP (5)
  7th Rule #28 OSS (1, 3, 5, 10)

12 **In Halls without permission or misuse of a hall pass**
  1st Detention (1)
  2nd Detention (2)
  3rd Saturday School (1)

13 **Minor Disruption and/or Removal from Class**
  1st OPS (1)
  2nd Saturday School (1)
  3rd ISACP (2)
  4th Rule #28, first available step on progression (1)
  5th Rule #28 (3)

14 **Leaving the Building without Permission**
  1st Saturday School (1)
  2nd ISACP (1)
  3rd ISACP (3)
  4th ISACP (5)
  5th Rule #28 OSS

15 **Use of Inappropriate Language (directed at staff automatic 5-day OSS)**
  1st OPS (1)
  2nd ISACP (1)

  4th ISACP (3)
  5th ISACP (5)
  6th Rule #28 OSS (1, 3, 5, 10)

20 **Honors Violation**
  1st ISACP (1)
  2nd ISACP (3)
  3rd ISACP (5)
  4th Rule #28 OSS (1, 3, 5, 10)

21 **Injurious Behavior**
  1st ISACP (1)
  2nd ISACP (3)
  3rd ISACP (5)
  4th Rule #28 OSS (1, 3, 5, 10)

22 **Violation of Acceptable Use Policy**
  Administrative Discretion

23 **Trespassing**
  Administrative Discretion

24 **Disobedience to Administrative Direction**
  1st OSS (3)
  2nd OSS (5)
  3rd OSS (7)
  4th Rule #48
       OSS (10) with Recommendation for Expulsion

25 **Misuse of Facilities and Equipment**
  Administrative Discretion

(Continued)

(Continued)

NAME OF HIGH SCHOOL
DISCIPLINE CONSEQUENCES GRID (School Year)

26. **Commission of any of the acts of misconduct specified in Section II of this policy, dealing with grounds for expulsion**

27. **Failure to Complete Minor Disciplinary Sanctions**
    Administrative Discretion (Missing Saturday School: One reschedule) OSS (1) after one reschedule

28. **Repeated Minor Violations**

EXPULSIONS

29. **Abusive, harassing, and/or disrespectful behavior**
    (Automatic OSS if directed at a staff member)
    Administrative Discretion

30. **Vandalism**
    Reflective of Seriousness of the Act

31. **Fireworks and Explosives**
    1st   OSS (10) with Recommendation for Expulsion

32. **Assault**
    1st   OSS (10) with Recommendation for Expulsion and Police Report

35. **Involvement with Alcoholic Beverages**
    1st   OSS (10) with Recommendation for Expulsion

36. **Involvement with Drugs and Drug Paraphernalia**
    1st   OSS (10) with Recommendation for Expulsion

37. **Theft of School or Private Property/ possession of stolen property**
    1st   OSS (3)
    2nd OSS (5)
    3rd   OSS (7)
    4th   OSS (10) with Recommendation for Expulsion
    Lunch ISACP (3)

38. **Arson/Attempted Arson/ Possession of Incendiary Device**
    1st   OSS (10) with Recommendation for Expulsion

39. **Disruption of School**
    A. **MINOR**
       OPS- Refer to Class Disruption
    B. **MAJOR**
       OSS (1-10)

40. **Extortion**
    Administrative Discretion (Reflective of Seriousness of the Act)

43. **Hazing**
    Administrative Discretion (Reflective of Seriousness of the Act)

44. **Violation of Board of Education Policies or School Rules and Regulations**
    Administrative Discretion (Reflective of Seriousness of the Act)

45. **Sexual Harassment**
    Administrative Discretion (Reflective of Seriousness of the Act)

46. **Failure to Provide Evidence/ Providing False Information/ Lying**
    (Reflective of Seriousness of the Act)
    1st   ISACP (3)
    2nd ISACP (5)
    3rd   OSS (1)
    4th   OSS (3)
    5th   OSS (5)
    6th   OSS (10) with Recommendation for Expulsion

47. **Sexual Conduct**
    1st   OSS (10) with Recommendation for Expulsion

48. **Repeated or Continued Violation of Minor School Conduct or Rules for which Suspension May Be Imposed**

33 **Fighting**
   1st OSS (5)
   2nd OSS (10) with Recommendation for Expulsion

34 **Involvement with weapons or dangerous instruments**
   1st OSS (10) with Recommendation for Expulsion

41 **Make False Fire Alarms and Bomb Threats**
   1st OSS (10) with Recommendation for Expulsion

42 **Violation of Local, State, or Federal Laws**
   Administrative Discretion (Reflective of Seriousness of the Act)

Figure B.5. Discipline Consequences Grid

CLASSROOM DISCIPLINE PLAN

It is important for all staff to develop a classroom plan to reflect the school philosophy on discipline. All staff should complete their Discipline Plan, turn into the office, share with students and parents and post in their classroom.

Room Rules (no more than 5 rules stated positively)
1.
2.
3.
4.
5.

Classroom Procedures (list procedures often used)
1.
2.
3.
4.
5.

Consequences for not following classroom rules
1.
2.
3.
4.

Positive methods used to promote student self-esteem
1.
2.
3.
4.

Figure B.6. Classroom Discipline Plan K–8

CLASSROOM MANAGEMENT PLAN ASSESSMENT

Name   Course

The following items are suggested requirements for effective Classroom Management Plans and serve as a reasonable template for review. Items listed below should be included in your management plan. Please spend time reviewing and preparing the Classroom Management Plan that you will be distributing to your class next year. Remember, this is the first impression students, parents and guardians will have of you and your expectations.

Course Description and Objectives
Student Supplies: Special requirements and/or daily materials needed for class
Grading Policy
Grading criteria and how grades will be calculated
Extra Credit Policy
Tests and Quizzes

Make up work (follow the school policy in the student/parent handbook)
    Expectation that students will write assignments in the student handbook/planner
    Classroom Expectations and Rules
    Specific standard operating procedures for the class
    Hall Pass Policy
    Expectations for behavior, cooperation, and safety
    Classroom discipline plan including consequences for violations
    Consequences for class tardiness
    How Parents Can Reach You
    How to contact the teacher (school phone number, voice mail, e-mail)
    How students should seek extra help

Disclaimer: "This is not meant to be all encompassing. As the year progresses, there may be a need for additional assignments or modifications to expectations."
    Parent and Student Signatures. This section indicates that the parent/guardian and student have read and understood the terms of the plan.
    This is a new Classroom Management Plan.
    This Classroom Management Plan was approved and used last year, however, changes have been made and have been highlighted.
    This Classroom Management Plan was approved and used last year—no changes have been made.
    Reviewed by:
    Assistant Principal/**Principal**   Date:
    Approved as is, nice work.
    Revise and return a copy to my mailbox.

Figure B.7.   Classroom Management Plan Assessment

DISCIPLINE INCIDENT REPORT FORM

Teacher/Principal Filling Out Report: Position:

Name of Individual(s) Making Report:

Date of Incident: Time of Incident:

Location of Incident:

Student(s) Initiating Infraction: Student(s) Affected: Witnesses:

Type of Incident:

Comments by person completing report:

Copy of Report Given to Administrator:

Name:

Date: Time:

FOLLOW UP (To be Filled Out by Administration):

Name:

Parents Contacted: YES NO   <u>Date:</u>   <u>Time:</u>

Response::

Incident Report (To be Completed by Student/Witness):

Please report what happened in your own words:

_____
_____
_____
_____
_____
_____
_____
_____
_____
_____
_____
_____

When/Where Did This Happen:

_____
_____
_____

What Steps Have Been Taken to Resolve this Situation (if any) completed by teacher/principal:

_____
_____
_____
_____

Print Name: _____   Signature _____
Date: _____   Time: _____

Figure B.8. Discipline Incident Report

Appendix B

PRINCIPAL'S GOOD NEWS CALL

In an effort to promote positive reinforcement in our school, staff and students can be nominated to receive a positive call from the principal to recognize their efforts.

This award is to certify that

_____
Student's Name

Has been nominated for a call from the principal by

_____
Teacher or Staff Signature

For the following reasons:

_____

_____

Congratulations for a job well done!

_____   _____
Principal's Signature   Date

Figure B.9.   Principal's Good News Calls

MASTER SCHEDULE CHART

ID	Task Name	Duration (days)	Start	Finish	Resource Name
1	New Course Proposals	16	Mid Aug	End Aug	Dept. Chairs
2	Review New Course Proposals	7	Mid Sept	Mid Sept	Principal
3	Program of Studies Recommendations	5	Mid Sept	Eng Sept	Dept. Chairs
4	Review New Course Proposals with Central Office	7	Late Sept	Early Oct	Principal & Superintendent
5	Present New Courses to BOE	1	Early Oct	Early Oct	Principal
6	Review Program Studies Changes	14	Mid Oct	Late Oct	Administrators, Dept. Chairs & HS Guidance
7	Program Studies Typed	15	Late Oct	Mid Nov	Principal's secretary
8	Program Studies Printed & Placed Online	16	Mid Nov	Beg Dec	Principal's secretary
9	Course Selection Sheets Developed & Printed	21	Mid Dec	Early Jan	Assistant Principal & HS Guidance
10	Team Review of Updated Course Selection Sheets	6	Early Jan	Mid Jan	Assistant Principal & HS Guidance
11	8th Grade Parent Night	1	Mid Jan	Mid Jan	Principal, Assistant Principal & HS Guidance
12	Program of Studies Copies to Learwood & St. Joe's	1	Late Jan	Late Jan	HS Guidance
13	Learwood Scheduling Info Visit	1	Late Jan	Late Jan	Principal, Assistant Principal, Guidance, and Athletic Director
14	Schedule Info Visit St. Joes	1	Late Jan	Late Jan	Principal, Assistant Principal, Guidance, and Athletic Director
15	Learwood Mock Scheduling Day St. Joe's Mock Scheduling Day	2	Early Feb	Early Feb	HS Guidance
16	Learwood Recommendation Day	1	Early Feb	Early Feb	MS Guidance
17	Learwood Course Selection Sheets Returned to MS	7	Early Feb	Mid Feb	MS Guidance
18	9th Grade Scheduling Meeting 12th Period PAC	1	Mid Feb	Mid Feb	HS Guidance
19	10th Grade Scheduling Meeting 11th Period PAC	1	Mid Feb	Mid Feb	HS Guidance
20	11th Grade Scheduling Meeting 10th Period PAC	1	Mid Feb	Mid Feb	HS Guidance
21	HS Course Recommendation Day HR AM & PM	1	Late Feb	Late Feb	Assistant Principal & Guidance
22	HS Guidance Review and Student Enter Course Requests	7	Late Feb	Late Feb	HS Guidance

#	Task	Days	Start	End	Responsible
23	HS Course Selection Sheets Returned with Parent Sig.	1	Late Feb	Late Feb	HS Guidance
24	Learwood Course Selection Sheets Student Entered	16	Late Feb	Mid-March	HS Guidance
25	Develop Course Needs From Student Request Data	6	Mid-March	Mid-March	Principal and Assistant Principals
26	Final Day for 10/11/12 Grades to appeal class recommendations	1	Late March	Late March	Administrators & HS Guidance
27	Finalize HS Teaching Staff Needs Based On Data	5	Late March	Late March	Principal and Assistant Principals
28	Final Approval Teacher Needs By Central Office	12	Mid March	Late March	Principal & Superintendent
29	Department Input on Teaching Assignments	3	Late March	Late March	Dept. Chairs
30	Master Schedule Creation (2 Days)	2	Late March	Late March	Principal, Assistant Principals, and HS Guidance
31	Build Master Schedule Input Master Schedule Run Simulations	28	Late March	Late April	Principal, Assistant Principals, and HS Guidance
32	Final Day for 9th Graders to appeal class recommendations	1	Early May	Early May	Administrators & HS Guidance
33	Draft Master Schedule to Dept. Chairs for Input	4	Early May	Early May	Staff by department
34	Give Staff Tentative Teaching Assignments	1	Late May	Late May	Principal and Assistant Principals
35	Work On Remaining Schedueling Problems	33	Late May	Late June	Principal
36	Create & Mass Add Study Hall, Lab Study Halls	33	Late Mau	Late June	Assistant Principal
37	Type Final Draft Master Schedule & Distribute	5	Mid Aug	Mid Aug	Assistant Principal
38	Print Student Schedules	1	Mid Aug	Mid Aug	Office Staff

Figure B.10. Guidelines for Creating a Master Schedule

TEACHING ASSIGNMENT WORKSHEET

TEACHER NAME   <u>DEPARTMENT</u>

The following list of courses and the number of sections I will teach of each course was decided upon in a department meeting. My signature at the bottom signifies that I have agreed as part of a departmental process to teach the following courses for the school year.

	Course(s)	Number of sections
1		
2		
3		
4		
5		

Teacher Signature

Please list below the courses you would prefer to teach with number one as your first priority.

1.
2.
3.
4.
5.

Please list below all teaching certificates that you hold.

1.
2.
3.
4.

Figure B.11. Teaching Assignment Sheet

Appendix B

COMMITTEE EVALUATION

Please take the time to answer a few yes and no questions concerning our committee's workings this school year. Feel free to offer a narrative of any ideas you might have.

1. We receive the meeting agenda and materials in advance of the meeting to allow for appropriate review and preparation.
2. Our members come to meetings prepared and ready to contribute.
3. We use our meeting time well.
4. The members agree on the goals and directions of the committee.
5. Our leader is efficient and keeps the committee on task.
6. All members are encouraged to speak and contribute.
7. Something I like the most about being a part of this committee:
8. Something I think the committee could do to improve:
9. Something that the committee could focus on in the future:
10. Please add any other comments here.

Figure B.12. Committee Evaluation Form

Appendix C

REFERENCE CHECK FORM
Certified/Classified Personnel (Circle One)

Date:
NAME OF APPLICANT:
☐ **Former Employer**
☐ *Character Reference*
☐ Personal Reference

School District/Organization

Address *Phone*

Name of Person Contacted *Position/Title*

Relationship to Applicant:

1. What were the dates of his/her employment by your school district/organization?
   From   to
2. What was his/her position/title?
3. What can you tell me about the quality of his/her work?
4. Did he/she receive any promotions other than the standard step? Awards?
5. On a scale of 1–4, one being the lowest, how would you rate this candidate in the following areas:

Certified		Classified	
Assessment of skills & abilities	Rating	Assessment of skills & abilities	Rating
Knowledge of subject matter		Knowledge of position/job	
Classroom management		Management of resources	
Cooperation		Cooperation	
Rapport with students, staff, parents		Ability to work without supervision	
Punctuality		Punctuality	
Dependability		Dependability	
Loyalty		Loyalty	
Honesty		Honesty	
Integrity		Integrity	
Ethics		Ethics	
Oral communication skills		Oral communication skills	
Written communication skills		Written communication skills	
Hard worker		Work quality	
Ability to get along with others		Ability to get along with others	
Technology knowledge		Technology knowledge	

Figure C.1. Reference Check Form

INTERVIEW QUESTIONNAIRE FOR TEACHERS

Name of Candidate:

Date/Time:

Location:

Name of Interviewer:

Questions	Notes/comments	Rating 1 = Low — 5 = High
1. What are your qualifications (both academic and personal) for a teaching position at (NAME OF SCHOOL)		1 2 3 4 5
2. What would you do to foster good communication between school and the parents of students in your classroom?		1 2 3 4 5
3. How will you provide for individual differences (both developmental and academic)?		1 2 3 4 5

Questions	Notes/comments	Rating 1 = Low — 5 = High
4. What is your philosophy of discipline? What would you do to establish and maintain a positive learning environment?		1 2 3 4 5
5. Describe a good lesson (in your major field).		1 2 3 4 5
6. What behavior(s) do you exhibit which would convince students that you enjoy teaching?		1 2 3 4 5
7. A. Using a word or phrase, describe your three greatest strengths. B. Using a word or phrase, describe three areas in which you would like to grow professionally.		1 2 3 4 5
8. Are you interested in coaching or other co-curricular activities?		1 2 3 4 5
9. What professional activities do you plan to be involved in, over the next one to three years, which will increase your knowledge and expertise?		1 2 3 4 5
10. What is your experience with technology?		1 2 3 4 5

Figure C.2. Interview Questionnaire for Teachers

Name of School
PROFESSIONAL DEVELOPMENT RECORD

Staff Member:

Organization memberships/offices:

Workshops/conferences/courses/presentations, etc.

School events attended:

Extracurricular activities:

Cooperative initiatives with colleagues:

District-level involvement (e.g., committees):

Parent contacts/conferences:

Other school-related or community accomplishments:

HIGHLIGHTS

Please list below creative lessons that you do during a certain time of the year that you are proud of. Please include any lessons that support our Professional Learning Communities work.

September

October

November

December

January

February

March

April

May

June—August

Figure C.3. **Professional Development Record**

Teacher	Due date Professional Growth Conference	Pre-Conference #1	Due date Observation #1	Post Conference #1	Walkthrough #1	Walkthrough #2	Observation #2	Pre-Conference #2	Post Conference #2	Due date

Figure C.4. Teacher Evaluations Chart

END OF YEAR CHECK-OUT LIST

NAME:

Listed below are the items and articles that must be checked off (initialed) prior to your exit interview.

The following must be turned in and initialed by **(Head Custodian).**

    Room secured and checked by Head Custodian

    Custodial Work Orders

    Summer Maintenance Request forms

    Key Inventory & Visual Check of I.D.

The following must be completed and checked off and initialed by the **Department Chair:**

    Textbooks returned to the proper room

    Textbook Inventory Sheet for your classes

    One blank copy of your final exam and KEY

    Supply Orders

The following must be turned in and initialed by the **Department Chair of Guidance:**

    Student Failure Lists or Retentions

These items must be turned in and checked off by the following administrator or assistant during your exit interview before you leave the building for the summer on your last workday:

Assistant Principal or Administrative Secretary or Lead Teacher:

    List of incompletes that have not been changed with attached explanations

    Textbook Inventory

    Rebind Inventory Sheet (Department chairs only)

    Emergency Response Plan

Assistant Principal or Administrative Secretary or Lead Teacher:

    IEP cover sheets

    All blank forms, i.e., detentions, passes, etc.

    Clear Hall Passes

    Incomplete and Missing Grades

Principal: (AFTER ALL OTHER AREAS ABOVE HAVE BEEN INITIALED)

    Teacher Professional Development Form (Goals for the next school year)

    Grade Book/Attendance Records—put ▶ your name ▶ school year ▶ periods and ▶ classes on the front cover with a key inside.

All final exams with ▶teacher name ▶class and ▶period(s) on the cover.

Makeup Final Exams (bundled neatly) including ▶student name ▶class period and ▶teacher name

Classroom Management Plan or Classroom Discipline Plan for approval

This End of Year Checklist, initialed by Head Custodian, Department Chair, Guidance Department Chair, Assistant Principals or Administrative Lead Teacher

All teachers must sign out in the principal's secretary's office on the last day of school.

Principal's secretary:

Time signed out of the building:

Summer phone number:

Summer e-mail:

Figure C.5. End of Year Check-Out List

Appendix D

	ADMINISTRATIVE GOALS		
Goal statement:	Correlating principal standard	Measure/evidence (Products):	Degree met (full, partial, not)

GOALS SHOULD INCLUDE:
— Evidence that includes learning
— Measures of personal/professional learning and growth
— Building/department-wide improvement

Figure D.1.   Administrative Goals

BASIC PRINCIPLES OF ELEMENTARY LIFE

1. Invest in EVERY relationship. They Matter!

2. CHOOSE YOUR WORDS! They ALWAYS have power.

3. Celebrate the victories!

4. COMMUNICATE! It can be the bridge between confusion and clarity.

5. Positivity is a *choice*. It all begins and ends *in your mind*.

6. Be intentional EVERY day. We all can GROW!

7. LOVE your students, even during the toughest moments.

Figure D.2.   Basic Principles of Elementary Life

IMPROVING COMMUNICATION

Item	Talking Points	Student specific notes
Welcome	Introduction of people in the meeting (or on the call) and their roles in supporting	
Attendance	Give a narrative of attendance patterns observed in your subject area	ELA Math Science
	Homeroom teacher: Discuss HB 410 as needed	SS Specials
Participation	What is the in-class participation like?	ELA
	What does out-of-class contact look like?	Math Science SS Specials
Performance	In-class performance	ELA
	Report Card analysis	Math
	Test data	Science SS Specials
Home-learning	What are the home logistics?	*For example:*
	Homeroom teacher: What are some ways the school could remove hurdles for home learning?	Daycare/home? Learning space? Siblings? Times of day? Live/Asynchronous?
Strengths and Weaknesses	What are the parent's perceived strengths/weaknesses of the student?	ELA Math Science
	What about the student's perceptions?	SS Specials
Moving Forward	Goal setting for student improvement	ELA
	Summarize action items for all parties.	Math
	Make any deadlines clear and document.	Science SS
	Make communication expectations of each party clear.	Specials
Follow up	Schedule any follow ups needed. Send invites.	
Open Questions	Does the parent have any lingering concerns?	

Figure D.3. Improving Communication

Appendix D

ELEMENTARY SCHOOL MISSION STATEMENT

Our Elementary School is a learning partnership dedicated to encouraging high achievement and lifelong learners.

Norms

At Our Elementary, *we are committed* **to the following norms:**

- Listen and be an active participant.
- Work as a team to problem solve.
- Be on time, prepared, accountable, and on task.
- Be flexible, willing to listen, and share ideas.
- Have an agenda, take and share minutes.
- Have a positive attitude.

Core Beliefs

At Our Elementary, we believe:

- Teachers make a critical difference in motivating and inspiring students for success.
- Positive visions and collaboration are essential for success.
- All children have talents, skills, and unique abilities.

Commitments

At Our Elementary, *we are committed* **to the following best practices:**

- Rigorous instruction.
- Collaborative planning time for grade levels.
- Differentiating instruction and assessments based on student needs.
- Conferencing with students about their progress.
- Writing across the curriculum.

Figure D.4. **Elementary School Mission Statement and Beliefs**

Guidance Department Overview & Alignment of Guidance Responsibilities

9th Grade	10th Grade	11th Grade	12th Grade
Name of Counselor	Name of Counselor	Name of Counselor	Name of Counselor**
Shared Assistant Principals	One Assistant Principal	One Assistant Principal	One Assistant Principal
1) Transition 8th graders to 9th Grade (attend meetings)	1) Alternative Program students in caseload	1) College/Career Resource Room (secure materials)	1) Senior College Applications
2) Work with "Success" classes to transition 9th graders to HS	2) 504 Accommodation Plans for caseload	2) Schedule College Visits	2) Select tasks for Scholarship Fair/Senior Dessert (shared)
3) 504 Accommodation Plans for caseload	3) HS Credit Flex courses for caseload	3) Scholarship Fair/Senior Dessert (shared)	3) Post-Secondary Educational Options & College Credit Plus
4) HS Credit Flex for caseload	4) PSAT-Preliminary Scholastic Aptitude Test for 10th graders & State Graduation Tests (shared)	4) Vocational Program (oversee present 11th graders)	4) Education Management Information System (EMIS) Codes
5) Testing Coordinator—Includes: Preliminary Scholastic Aptitude Test (PSAT) & Advanced Placement (AP) All grades	5) Credit Recovery (Summer coursework)	5) Alternative Program students in caseload	5) Alternative Program: Enter grades & credits on all student transcripts
6) State Graduation Testing (shared)	6) Dual Credit for caseload	6) 504 Accommodation Plans for caseload	6) 504 Accommodation Plans for caseload
7) National Assessment of Educational Progress (NAEP) Test	7) Bullying Prevention Program	7) HS Credit Flex courses for caseload	7) HS Credit Flex for caseload
8) National Collegiate Athletic Association Eligibility (shared)	8) Career Based Intervention	8) Dual Credit for caseload	8) Dual Credit for caseload
9) Measure of Academic Progress (MAP) Tests if given	9) Vocational Program Liaison	9) National Collegiate Athletic Association Eligibility (shared)	9) Assist with Master Schedule
10) Vocational Program—College Fair (shared)	10) Duty (12 weeks)	10) Assist with Master Schedule	10) Free Application for Federal Student Aid (FAFSA) night
11) Duty (12 weeks)		11) Graduation Test Intervention (Summer—11th/12th Grades)	11) Duty (12 weeks)
		12) Duty (12 weeks)	

**Senior Guidance Counselor stipend

Figure D.5. Guidance Department Overview

City Schools
High School

Phone: Fax:

   Building Principal
   Assistant Principal
   Assistant Principal

PROXIMITY CONTRACT

I,   will not be in close proximity with:

due to differences that cannot be resolved. I will not communicate with the said student unless there is an emergency, or an academic reason that would require me to do so.

Furthermore, I will not have physical contact with or mention the name of

in written notes, conversation, communications, hearsay, or gossip due to previous allegations and confrontations regarding the conditions stated in this contract.

I will not encourage, entice, or coerce other classmates to engage in any of the above activity on my behalf toward the other.

The staff and faculty of   High School are aware of this contract and will assist in the monitoring and enforcement of this agreement.

Failure to comply with the statements and conditions above will result in punitive consequences to the highest degree appropriate:

1st offense—3 day OSS
2nd offense—5 day OSS
3rd offense—7 day OSS with a recommendation for expulsion

Student (acknowledging)   *Student (affected)*

Administrator   *Date*

Figure D.6.   Proximity Contract

References

Bransford, John D. and Barry Stein. *Ideal Problem Solver: A Guide for Improving Thinking, Learning and Creativity*. New York: W.H. Freeman and Company, 1999.

Brown-Chidsey, Rachel and Mark W. Steege. *Response to Intervention: Principles and Strategies for Effective Practices*. New York: Guilford Press, 2005.

Brainy Quotes.com. "Mother Teresa Quotes." BrainyMedia Inc, 2020. www.brainyquote.com/quotes/mother_teresa_133195, accessed June, 2020.

Brainy Quotes.com. "Theodore Roosevelt Quotes." BrainyMedia Inc, 2020. www.brainyquote.com/quotes/theodore_roosevelt_380703, accessed June, 2020.

Covey, Stephen R. *Principle-Centered Leadership*. New York: Fireside, 1992.

DuFour, Richard and Rebecca and Robert Eaker. *Whatever It Takes; How Professional Learning Communities Respond When Kids Don't Learn*. Bloomington, Indiana: Solutions Tree, 2004.

Rath, Tom and Mary Reckmeyer. *How Full is Your Bucket for Kids*. Washington D.C.: Gallup Press, 2009.

Schoenlein, James J. "Intervention Assistance Teams in Ohio: From Where? To Where?" *American Secondary Education*, Vol. 20, No 2 (1991):27–30.

About the Author

Dr. Janet M. Litzel is a native of Ohio having earned her BS in Elementary Education at Kent State University and her MS and Ed.D. in Educational Administration from the University of Akron. Dr. Litzel is an experienced school administrator having served as an elementary and middle school teacher and principal in Ohio for over twenty-six years. As a building administrator, she was recognized by the Ohio Association of Elementary Schools Administrators and the Ohio Middle School Association for outstanding performance.

While serving as a middle school principal, Dr. Litzel's experience in higher education began in 1991 when she joined the faculty at the University of Akron as an adjunct professor in educational administration. Following her retirement from public school administration in 1996, she joined the full-time faculty at the University of Akron in the Department of Curriculum, and Instruction and Educational Administration. Dr. Litzel later served as a Director of Student Teaching and implemented the Professional Development School program for the university's College of Education.

Dr. Litzel continued her higher education teaching through online graduate instruction for both the University of Akron and Ashland University in the areas of Curriculum and instruction and Educational Administration. She is currently a graduate instructor for Cleveland State University in the Center for Educational Leadership teaching Policy and Planning and School Operations and Personnel Management.

Dr. Joanie A. Walker is a native of Ohio having earned her BS in Business Education and her MS and Ed.D. in Educational Administration from the University of Akron. Dr. Walker has over thirty years of experience as an educator and twenty-one years as a secondary school administrator. She is the only two-time Ohio High School Principal of the Year.

Since 2016, Dr. Walker has served as a Professor of Practice for the Counseling Administration Supervision and Adult Learning Department at Cleveland State University. In her role as Professor of Practice, she serves as an instructor and advisor for Master's and Doctorate students in school administration. She is also a Coach for the Institute for Premier Leadership, a member of the Ohio Principal Preparation Program Committee, and assists with the Education Policy Fellowship Program for Cleveland State University's Center for Educational Leadership principal's program.

Dr. Walker is an active member of OASSA (Ohio Association of Secondary School Administrators) and NASSP (National Association of Secondary School Principals) where she has been a presenter on a variety of topics for aspiring administrators, assistant principals, and principals. Her doctoral dissertation focused on positive school climate, communication, and female leadership.

www.ingramcontent.com/pod-product-compliance
Lightning Source LLC
Chambersburg PA
CBHW052049300426
44117CB00012B/2045